Chai
Learning for Jewish Life

Second Grade Curriculum Core

UAHC Press
New York, New York

Printed on acid-free paper
Copyright © 2002 by UAHC Press
Manufactured in the United States of America
10 9 8 7 6 5 4 3 2 1

UNION OF AMERICAN HEBREW CONGREGATIONS

Rabbi Eric H. Yoffie *President*
Rabbi Daniel H. Freelander *Vice President*
Rabbi Jan D. Katzew, RJE, Ph.D. *Director, Department of Jewish Education*
Kenneth Gesser *Publisher, UAHC Press*
Rabbi Hara Person *Editorial Director, UAHC Press*

Contributors

Alan J. Levin, Ph.D. *Project Director*
Joanne Doades, M.A.R.E., *Education Project Specialist*
Federica K. Clementi, Ph.D. *Project Editor*
Faye Tillis Lewy, z"l *Project Consultant*

Authors

Michelle Shapiro Abraham, MAJE, RJE *Family Education*
Keren Alpert *Temple Boards and Education Committee Guides*
Lisa Lieberman Barzilai, MAJE, RJE *Curriculum Core*
Irene Bolton *Curriculum Core*
Joanne Doades, M.A.R.E. *Early Childhood Parent Education*
Deborah Gettes *Curriculum Core*
Melanie Cole Goldberg, MAJE, MAJCS, RJE *Curriculum Core*
Debbie Joseph *Curriculum Core*
Barbara Binder Kadden, MAJE, MAJCS, RJE *Parent Education*
Martha Katz, M.A. *Early Childhood Parent Education*
Alan J. Levin, Ph.D. *Early Childhood Parent Education*
Lesley Litman, M.A. *Curriculum Core*
Marlene Myerson, MEd, RJE *Curriculum Core*
Deborah Niederman, MAJE, RJE *Curriculum Core*
Renee B. Rittner, MAJE, MSW *Teacher Training*
Cheri Ellowitz Silver, MAJE, MAJCS, M.S.Ed., RJE *Mitkadem Hebrew Program*
Lesley Silverstone, MAJE, RJE *Teacher Training*

Academic Advisors

Isa Aron, Ph.D., RJE *Teacher Training*
Lisa Grant, Ph.D. *Parent Education*
Rabbi Sam Joseph, RJE *Temple Boards and Education Committee Guides*
Jo Kay, M.A. *Family Education and Early Childhood Parent Education*
Sara Lee, MAJE, M.S.Ed., RJE *Mitkadem Hebrew Program*
Michael Zeldin, Ph.D, RJE *Curriculum Core*

NATE Readers*

Lori L. Abramson, MAJE, RJE
Judith V. Aronson, MTS, RJE
Birgit R. Anderson, MAJE, RJE
Tirza Arad
Alan D. Bennett, FRE, RJE
Deena Bloomstone, MAJE, RJE
Sherry Blumberg, Ph.D., RJE
Debra Colodny
Mindy B. Davids, MAJE, RJE
Itzik Eshel, Ph.D.
Robin Eisenberg, MEd, RJE
Terri Ginsburg, MEd
Abra Greenspan
Sharon Halper
Rabbi Vered Harris, MAJE
Ava Keenen, MEd
Julie Lambert, MAJE, RJE
Deborah Niederman, MAJE, RJE
Fran Pearlman, M.A., RJE
Roslyn Roucher, MAJE, RJE
Mona Senkfor, RJE
Rabbi Peretz Wolf-Prusan

*As of 06/02

Feldman Library

Table of Contents

G'MILUT CHASADIM

Introduction

The Jewish sages teach us that "the world stands on three things: *Torah, Avodah,* and *G'milut Chasadim,*" (*Avot 1:2*). These pursuits—study, worship, and deeds of loving-kindness—provide the framework within which Jews build their relationship with God, with one another, and with the world. Accordingly, *Torah, Avodah,* and *G'milut Chasadim* serve as the "core" of the *CHAI: Learning for Jewish Life* curriculum, providing students with the foundation for a lifetime of Jewish learning and living.

The students who sit before you in classrooms are children whose world is defined by more than just their formal Jewish educational experiences. They learn first and foremost from their parents, and many Jewish parents find it increasingly challenging to create a Jewish home and impart Jewish values to their children. Congregational schools can be a valuable partner in the process of strengthening Jewish family life.

The *CHAI* educational initiative addresses Jewish learning as a lifelong pursuit. The Union of American Hebrew Congregations has designed a full program of family and parent education sessions to enhance the ability to grow as Jewish adults and to create a home environment that will complement children's school-based learning.

This *CHAI* curriculum core contains 27 complete one-hour classroom lessons in *Torah, Avodah,* and *G'milut Chasadim.* A thirty-week-long school year will still allow a congregation to devote the remaining three school days to family education sessions.* The parent education sessions enable parents to be addressed as an adult cohort: therefore, incorporating up to three of these lessons every year is strongly recommended. This approach can provide a wonderful Reform model for parents and children learning and growing together.

*Each strand is meant to be taught as nine consecutive lessons. However, the order of the strands is flexible.

RECOMMENDED SAMPLE YEAR PROGRAM

	SUBJECT	NUMBER OF LESSONS
THROUGHOUT ONE SCHOOL YEAR	*Torah*	9 Sessions
	Avodah	9 Sessions
	G'milut Chasadim	9 Sessions
	Family Education Program	3 Sessions
	Parent Education Program	2 or 3 Sessions

Chai Lessons

The program has been developed following the Association for Supervision and Curriculum Development (ASCD) quality curriculum model known as "Understanding by Design." This approach, and that of *CHAI: Learning for Jewish Life* curriculum core, ensures that student learning will go beyond the specific classroom activities and will reach a deeper enduring understanding, which will establish the basis for later Jewish learning and living.

The curriculum core lessons are structured in two sections: one specifically for the teacher and the second one for class activities with the students. In the first part of a lesson the teacher will find a brief introduction that specifies the preparation needed to effectively run the class. This is followed by the actual lesson, which gives detailed information on what to ask students to lead them to a full understanding of the lesson's topic, class exercises, games, reading activities, and much more.

The following are some of the main sections into which the lessons are divided:

Introduction

Historical and cultural background, special instructions, overview of the lesson.

Enduring Understanding

Foundational concepts for Jewish learning. In some cases, a single "enduring understanding" applies to several lessons or to an entire unit.

Essential Questions

Inquiries leading to the enduring understandings.

Questions to be Addressed

These can be "triggers" that relate to the specifics of the lesson's message and can be a helpful guide to motivate the students to follow the process of the lesson.

Evidence of Understanding

The "evidence" of understanding assesses the success of the lesson from the students' perspective. (This "evidence" can be expressed orally, in writing, or demonstrated by a positive response in a student's behavior.)

Materials Needed

A listing of all materials and resources needed to execute the lesson.

New Vocabulary

Translations and clear explanations of Hebrew, Yiddish, and English words and expressions that are central to the understanding of a lesson's topic.

Activity Plan

Under "Activity Plan" are listed and defined all exercises and activities that constitute the actual lesson.

Set Induction

Ideas or questions that will lead the students from what is familiar and known to them to new, more abstract concepts.

Learning Activities

A series of activities—including readings, questions, role play, construction, and art—designed to bring back the abstract into the real-life realm the students can easily grasp and relate to.

Conclusion

Reflective wrap-up that reinforces the comprehension, uncovers misunderstandings, and shows whether the desired learning has taken place.

Homework

Light home activities that present an opportunity for reinforcing and extending the learning while involving other family members in the student's study.

CHAI: My Jewish Life Journal

Homework assigned at the end of class will be completed at home in the *Chai: My Jewish Life Journal*. The three sections of the journal, the *Torah Journal*, the *Avodah Workbook*, and the *G'milut Chasadim Diary*, include some of the texts and prayers studied in class for students to keep and for parents to review when helping the children with their assignments.

How To Make This Curriculum Work Best For You

Teachers may choose to use this book by grade, scheduling each of the total 27 lessons (nine per curriculum core strand: *Torah, Avodah,* and *G'milut Chasadim*) into their classroom time throughout a school year. The lessons can also be used by strand, to supplement one or two of the core areas of an existing curriculum. By selecting specific lessons one may support or enhance the curriculum already in use in a congregational school. The program's fullest potential is reached when used as designed (i.e., throughout a year duration by grade), but choosing to adopt only individual lessons can deeply heighten the excellence of school curricula.

JUMP RIGHT IN!

To ensure both the educational quality and the classroom viability of this curriculum, these *CHAI* curriculum core lessons were developed by different teams of Jewish educators in consultation with faculty specialists from Hebrew Union College–Jewish Institute of Religion, and reviewed by members of the National Association of Temple Educators. All that is left for teachers to do is:

- Read a lesson once or twice.

- Consider possible variations you might want to add to personalize the lessons for your classroom's needs.

- Jump right in and teach!

Questions? Contact your regional educator or the UAHC Department of Jewish Education at 212.650.4110, or write to educate@uahc.org.

Torah

Lisa Lieberman Barzilai and Lesley Litman

Foreword

Welcome to the world of Torah! We hope that you will find the following lessons fun, interesting, intriguing, and relevant for your students' lives. The goal of the Torah strand of the *CHAI: Learning for Jewish Life* Curriculum Core is to enable students to draw direct connections between Torah study and their lives—as suggested by the name itself of this unique education program. The scope of this Torah teaching is not the simple telling of the biblical stories. In designing this curriculum, we were less concerned with the students' ability to retell a particular event narrated in the Torah than with the possibility for them to ground an understanding, decision, or behavior in their study of the text. For example, in one of the following lessons ("*Parashat Bo*," units 4 and 5) students are asked to determine one special place in their home and to mark it with a mezuzah that they will have created as part of that lesson. This curriculum will have been successful if, every so often, the children will associate the mezuzah with the memory of that special place they have chosen—a cherished place in their homes, and therefore in their lives.

The overarching theme of our enduring understandings is that Torah study is a lifelong and ongoing process. To that end, the questions raised by the lessons and the discussions are open-ended and capable of sustaining multiple interpretations and directions.

The lessons are organized following the order of the Torah portions (*parshiyot*) in the Book of Exodus (*Sh'mot*) (the Torah consists of fifty-four portions, of which eleven are in the Book of *Sh'mot*). Each lesson focuses on one small aspect of a particular portion (*parashah*). The lessons are written with the understanding that students will study these portions and excerpts of Torah again and again in their lives and, at each encounter, they will find a new insight into the text. Therefore, teachers should not worry about whether the students remember each and every detail of the text or story contained in the lessons. There are two lessons for *Parashat Bo* that focus on the symbolism of the mezuzah. These are presented in the order in which the related verses appear in the Book of Exodus. They are, however, easily interchangeable, so teachers should feel free to choose the order that best suits their needs.

An exciting, and sometimes worrisome, aspect of Jewish teaching and learning is the nagging thought: "What if students ask something that I cannot answer?" We would like to reassure you that this is potentially a wonderful scenario. Students may ask some factual questions which will demand inquiry on the part of the teacher. Or they may raise some of those unanswerable questions, such as "Is God real?" All questions represent an opportunity to open new areas for dialogue and to engage in additional learning.

In creating these lessons, we had in mind those teachers without previous experience in teaching this type of Torah study. The following are some tips for those who are new to this process:

- Don't worry about not knowing the "right answer." More often than not there is no one correct answer. The beauty of Torah study is in the ability to pose multiple possibilities for understanding the same topic.

- Trust your life experience and your intuition as you respond to students' questions posed in the lesson plans.

- There is always more than one way to understand a given verse. Encourage your students to develop multiple perspectives and understandings whenever possible.

What "difficult" questions may the students ask a teacher? No one can predict for sure what kind of questions will come to the minds of attentive, curious second-graders. We tried to guess just a few and suggest only one of the many possible ways of answering your students' questions. Some examples may include:

IS THE TORAH TRUE?

We don't know. We are inclined to think, as Reform Jews, that the story of creation as told in the Book of Genesis is not true, but may be based on ancient legends. There is some evidence of historical truth in the Book of Exodus (*Sh'mot*) but there is no indication that it is historically accurate. There is a different kind of truth, however, in the Torah. This is the truth one finds in the lessons and insights it has for those who study it. The struggles of people and families, the challenges of making decisions and taking risks, the difficulty of following the rules—these ring true for all people. The "truth" is that there are many kinds of "truths," of which historical truth is only one possibility.

DID GOD WRITE THE TORAH?

We don't know for sure. There is some controversy about God's role in the redaction of the Bible. Some people say that God gave Moses the Torah or that God even dictated it word by word to him: some think that not Moses, but a number of writers were inspired by God in writing it. Others claim that, although filled with God's wishes and insights, the Bible wasn't dictated by God but originally thought of and realized by a human being. Most Reform Jews do not accept the theory of God dictating the Torah to Moses word by word, but subscribe to one of the other answers or to some combination of all of them.

DO I HAVE TO BELIEVE IN THE TORAH?

It's up to you—it's up to each of us. Perhaps more important than "believing" in the Torah is that you be open to what it has to say to you and how it can help you make decisions and figure out what to do in your life. (Here the teacher might want to give an example from the Torah lessons with regard to the insights it has for our lives).

HOW DO YOU KNOW THAT GOD EXISTS?

This is a wonderful question. When it comes to God-related questions, no one has the right, ultimate answer. We tend to believe that God exists because we see so many incredible things around us, so many wonders and beautiful creations, that we decide God is behind all this, that God exists and made everything possible. Why does the human body work? How do we begin to breathe when we are babies? What makes flowers grow? Where did the order of the world come from that makes day and night happen every day or the seasons come back each year? Some say the fact that we humans can tell right from wrong or can feel emotions is proof enough of God's existence. We can't ever know *who* God really is or *if* there is a God. We suggest that, whatever you decide, keep an open mind and an open heart to the very real possibility of God's existence.

DID GOD REALLY DO THESE THINGS?

We don't know. But why exclude this possibility? Even if God didn't do these things, the people who wrote the Torah certainly felt God's presence and wanted to express their closeness to God and their understanding of the role they believed God played in the creation of the world and of the Jewish people.

This is just a sample of what may come up during class. Indeed, this Torah curriculum is based on asking questions and finding as many answers as possible to each question.

As part of their discussions and activities, students will find many text elements they can relate to their daily experiences. Discussing in class is just as important as "covering" all the material in the lesson plan. These lessons are purposely chock-full—we preferred to give the teacher a lot, rather than too little, to work with. We recommend that teachers review each lesson with great care, consider their students' level and abilities, and determine whether all or only some of the activities would be appropriate for their classes. In some of the lessons you will find specific recommendations about what can be omitted in case of time limitation.

There are nine Torah lessons for second grade. The first is a general introduction to the Torah, the goal of which is to introduce the notion that Torah is a different type of book from those students encounter in their lives. The major focus of the Torah is to help us learn about how to live better lives. Then follows an introduction to the Book of *Sh'mot*, the focus of the remainder of the Torah strand. Students will have the opportunity to situate the Book of Exodus in the Torah as the second of the five books of the Torah. Students will be introduced to the names and themes of the eleven *parshiyot* that make up the book, as well as to a major theme of the book: Becoming a people. Students are not expected to memorize the names or number of portions. The goal is to introduce them to the concept of "*parashah*" (portion) and the general theme of the book.

The remaining seven lessons focus on six of the eleven portions of Exodus. The themes were chosen for their salience for second-graders and their potential to be carried beyond the classroom and into the students' lives. To facilitate this process, each lesson concludes with the opportunity for students to write or draw in their personal TORAH JOURNAL. Most of the homework is to be done at home in the hopes that the assignments will lead to interesting and important Jewish conversations between parents and children. We are also aware that second-grade students are at varying levels with regard to reading and writing. All of the activities in the Torah strand may be modified so that students do not have to write. We also strongly recommend the use of high school or parent aides in the classroom, both to help the teacher and as wonderful role models for the students.

We wish you, your students, and their families an enjoyable Torah experience full of learning and new understanding.

Introduction to Torah

Introduction: Lesson Overview

The Introduction to the Torah strand is essentially two lessons in one. The first part helps students focus on the "physical" attributes of the Torah scroll. Students will have the opportunity to compare a Torah scroll to a picture book or story book about creation. This will allow both teacher and students to explore what is special about the Torah to the Jewish people—both through examining how the Torah is "dressed" and how we, as Jews, use it each week.

The second part focuses on the notion that the Torah can teach us about our daily lives. The class will look at the opening story in the Torah, the genesis of creation, and the importance of God's creation and our responsibility in maintaining God's creations. Finally, the students will be assigned homework in their TORAH JOURNAL.

Enduring Understanding

➤ Torah is an ongoing dialogue between the text and its students.

➤ Torah is real in our daily lives; it is with us wherever we are.

➤ Developing the skills to study Torah is essential to integrating Torah into our lives.

Essential Questions

1. What does the Torah have to say to me and to my world?

2. Why is the Torah different from other books?

3. How can Torah study help me in my everyday life?

Questions to be Addressed

• How does the Torah differ from other books?

• What can the Torah teach us about our lives that will always remain with us?

- What is special about the Torah scroll?

- How is a Torah scroll different from a book that might deal with the same stories?

- Why is the Torah so important and special for the Jewish people?

- What can we learn from the Torah?

- What can the Torah teach us about our daily lives?

Evidence of Understanding

- Upon examination of the Torah scroll and a picture book, students will be able to describe how the Torah looks different from other books and what is special about it.

- Upon reading the story of creation from the Torah, students will be able to articulate that God is the Creator of all things.

- By "creating" their own imaginary animals, students will be able to articulate the importance of being a partner with God in maintaining our world.

Materials Needed

- Torah scroll

- Picture book of creation story

- Chalkboard and chalk or chart paper and marker

- Copies of the story of creation from the Torah

- "My Creation" handouts

- Pencils

- Crayons or markers

New Vocabulary

Aron Kodesh	*lit.* "Holy Ark": a cabinet (or a niche) in the synagogue where the Torah scrolls are kept.
Chumash	From the Hebrew word for "five," referring here to the first five books of the Torah. *Chumash* also indicates the book format (as opposed to handwritten scroll) in which the Torah can be published.

Genesis

Creation. The English name of the first book in the Torah. The word "genesis" is an ancient Greek word that literally means "to be born," to be created. (The Hebrew name for the Book of Genesis is "*B'reishit*" which in English means "at the beginning.")

sofer

lit. "scribe": the person in charge of handwriting Torah scrolls, scrolls for mezuzot and *t'fillin*, and other *m'gillot* (scrolls).

ACTIVITY PLAN

I.   Set Induction

Goal

- To show why and how the Torah is different from other books

Learning Activities

1. Place in front of the room a Torah scroll open to Genesis 1 (you can ask the rabbi, cantor, or educational director to help you find this section in the scroll) and an ordinary story book (ideally about creation) open to a page with illustrations.

2. Have the students describe what they see and point out the differences between the two books. Write them on the board or on chart paper.

    Students' comments might include:

    - One is in Hebrew and one in English.

    - One is handwritten and one is printed.

    - One is old and one is new.

    - One is a scroll and one is a book.

    - One is on parchment and one is on paper.

    - One has only words and one has words and pictures.

    What is similar about the two?

    Comments may include:

    - They both have words.

    - They both tell a story. (Or, they tell the same story.)

3. Ask the following question:

You might have already learned something about the Torah and heard about its great importance. Now that you have it in front of you, look at it and try to explain what makes the Torah special?

Comments may include:

- It tells the story of the Jewish people.
- It is *very* old.
- It is handwritten on a scroll.
- We dress it with special ornaments.
- We keep it in a special place, the *Aron Kodesh* (Holy Ark).
- It is written in Hebrew, the ancient language of the Jews.
- It has stories that can teach us about things in our own lives today.
- It is written by a *sofer* (scribe).
- We read it each week.

II. LEARNING ACTIVITIES

1. Read aloud for the class the creation story (see pp. 14–15).

   NOTE: The teacher might want to spare a moment to explain that the numbers next to each paragraph in the text refer to single verses contained within a chapter. It may be helpful to point out the verses in a *Chumash*.

2. After reading, explain to the students that the story they just heard is the same as the one handwritten in Hebrew on the Torah parchment in front of them.

3. Ask the following question: What different thing was created on each day?

   Day 1. Night and day

   Day 2. Sky (separation of heaven from earth)

   Day 3. Earth (dry land and water are separated)

   Day 4. Moon, stars, and sun

   Day 5. Birds and fish

Day 6. Animals and humans

Day 7. Shabbat*

*NOTE: The question of whether Shabbat was "created" (therefore, implying that work on Shabbat might be admissible) has long been debated by rabbis of all times and is far too complicated to be taught to second-graders. If students raise this question, though, the teacher might consider explaining—without getting into difficult philosophical details—that God's act of resting (God's not doing anything), made Shabbat (a word whose Hebrew root, שבת, means "rest") come into being.

4. Point out for the students the parallels between the first day and the fourth, the second and the fifth, the third and the sixth.

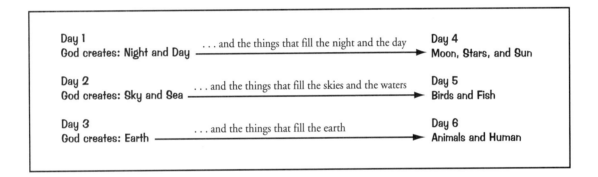

5. Ask students the following questions:

In Genesis 1:25–27 God gives humans the earth to rule and take care of. What do you think are our responsibilities as human beings regarding taking care of the earth?

Answers may include:

- Love, respect, and care for animals

- Love, respect, and care for plants

- Help provide food for those who are hungry and in need

- Don't litter or pollute the environment

- Recycle

What are some of the things you can do at home to show that you care for the animals and the plants?

Answers may include:

- Feed the pets

- Water the plants

- Walk the dog

- Play with my pet

What is the difference between taking care of your own pets or plants and taking care of someone else's pets or plants?

6. Read aloud for the students Genesis 2:19–20:

    Adonai formed out of the earth all the animals and all the birds, and brought them to Adam to see what he would call them; and whatever Adam called each living creature, that would be its name.

7. Give each student the sheet with the heading *My Creation*, found on page 17. Students will "create" their own animal. They will have to name the animal and give information about how to care for the animal. The creations will be shared with the class. As the students show the rest of the class their creations, you can ask them the following questions:

    - What do you think is special about the animal you created?

    - How would you feel if your animal actually existed? What would you want others to do to help keep your creation alive?

    - Is there something specific that made you want to create this animal? Why do you think it is different from any other existing creature?

8. Have the students look at the Torah again. Remind them that what has been done today in class is based on what the class read from the Torah. Have students answer the question: What did we learn from the Torah today?

    Answers may include:

    - that God created the universe

    - that God gave humans the responsibility to take care of the earth and everything on it

    - that we need to help take care of the earth and everything on it

    - that even though the Torah is old, written in Hebrew, and does not look like the books we are used to reading, it can teach us a lot about ourselves and our lives today

Conclusion

Make the conclusive connection for the students. Tell the students the following (rephrased as needed according to the specific needs of your class):

> By studying Torah, we can learn how to take care of the world. We can also learn how to live together in peace, and how to righteously conduct our daily lives. During the next few months we will be studying Torah together and learning how the Torah can help us to live our daily lives as human beings in general, and as Jews in particular.

Show the students a sample of the TORAH JOURNAL. This book has a page for each lesson of the Torah unit. It will be completed at home and will often involve a discussion between the student and his or her parent(s). The TORAH JOURNAL contains summaries of the various Torah stories or readings done in class for parents to see in order to be able to work at home with their child.

Explain to the students that this week they learned something from the Torah about life. Each week when they study Torah together in class, they will learn what Torah teaches about life. They will then go home and be a teacher to their family. Students will explain what they have learned in class and then with their parents, they will discuss the lesson and do another learning activity together. They will be both student and teacher at the same time.

Homework

1. Today we talked about the fact that we are partners with God in cherishing and protecting all that has been created. Discuss with your parent(s) how we are responsible for helping to keep God's creations safe. What is it that you do to help keep God's creations safe? (Taking care of a pet, recycling…)

2. When we study Torah, we are able to learn about our relationship to God, our relationship with other people and our relationship with the world. What do you and your parents hope to learn by studying Torah?

GENESIS

Chapter 1

1 When God began to create heaven and earth

2 The earth was unformed with darkness all around.

3 God said, "Let there be light," and there was light.

4 God saw that the light was good, and God separated the light from the darkness.

5 God called the light Day and the darkness God called Night. And there was evening and there was morning, a first day.

6 God said, "Let there be an expanse that separates water from water."

7 God made the expanse.

8 God called the expanse Sky. And there was evening and there was morning, a second day.

9 God said, "Let the water below the sky be gathered into one area, so the dry land will appear."

10 God called the dry land Earth, and the water God called Seas. And God saw that this was good.

11 And God said, "Let the earth sprout all types of plants." And it was so.

12 The earth sprouted every kind of plant and tree. And God saw this was good.

13 And there was evening and there was morning, a third day.

14 God said, "Let there be lights in the sky to separate day from night."

15 And it was so.

16 God made the two great lights, the greater light for the day and the lesser light for the night and stars.

17 God put them into the sky

18 To separate day and night, light from darkness. God saw that this was good.

19 There was evening and there was morning, a fourth day.

20 God said, "Let the waters have fish and the sky have birds."

21 God created the fish and birds. And God saw that this was good.

22 There was evening and there was morning, a fifth day.

23 God said, "Let the earth bring forth the animals." And it was so.

24 God made all the animals and creeping things on the earth. And God saw that this was good.

25 And God said, "Let us make humans in the image of God. They will rule over the fish, birds, animals and all the creeping things on earth."

26 And God created humans in the image of God.

27 God blessed them.

28 God said, "I give you every plant and tree for food.

29 And all the animals, birds and creeping things can use the plants for food." And it was so.

30 God saw all that was created and found it very good. And there was evening and morning, a sixth day.

Chapter 2

1 The heaven and earth were finished.

2 On the seventh day God finished the work of creation. God stopped from all of the work having been done.

3 God blessed the seventh day and declared it holy, because on it God stopped the work of creation.

Dear Parents:

Each week your children will receive an assignment to be completed in their TORAH JOURNAL. It is our belief that by studying Torah, we can learn how to better live and conduct our lives as Jews and as B'nai Adam (human beings). We suggest you take the time each week to sit down with your child and let him or her tell you what has been done and learned in school about Torah. This way your child will turn from student into teacher, and together your family will have the opportunity to share new learning. Some of the home assignments will also require your help and participation: these are all contained in the TORAH JOURNAL, where there are also Torah texts and readings included for you to get a better grasp of what we have done in class. As time goes on, you will find that the TORAH JOURNAL is a wonderful working and teaching tool to use with your child in examining, understanding, and cherishing the world around us.

Thank you for your important involvement in your child's study.

Sincerely,

_____

My Creation

Student's Name _____

Date _____

1. The name of my creation is _____

2. My creation lives in _____

3. I need to give my creation the following things for it to live well:_____

Introduction to the Book of *Sh'mot*

Introduction: Lesson Overview

This lesson is a two-part introduction to the entire Book of *Sh'mot* (Exodus). Part One points out where the Book of *Sh'mot* (the second book of the Torah) stands in relation to the other books. Students are asked to quickly flip through a *Chumash* (name of the Torah in its book format, not in the scroll form), finding the names of the five books of the Torah.

Part Two introduces the students to the concept of *parashah* (pl. *parshiyot*; Torah portion) and to the names and general themes of the *parshiyot* of the Book of *Sh'mot*—although students are not expected to memorize the names or themes of the *parshiyot*.

Part Two is divided into two activities:

A: The first activity will help students understand what it means, in their own lives, to become a group.

B: The second activity, building on the students' personal experiences, introduces them to the main theme of *Sh'mot,* the process of becoming a people. Every lesson in the Torah unit attempts to draw direct parallels between the experience of the Israelites and the experience of the students. The final section of Activity B tries to make a connection between the students' experience as articulated in Activity A and the Israelites' experience as addressed in Activity B.

Enduring Understanding

➤ Torah is an ongoing dialogue between the text and its students.

➤ Torah is real in our daily lives; it is with us wherever we are.

➤ Developing the skills to study Torah is essential to integrating Torah into our lives.

Essential Questions

1. What does the Torah have to say to me and to my world?

2. Why is the Torah different from other books?

3. How can Torah study help me in my everyday life?

Questions to be Addressed

- What are the five books of the Torah and which one will the class be studying?

- What is this book of the Torah about (main themes, storyline)?

- What is a *parashah*?

- How did the Israelites begin to be a people (group)?

- What can we learn about becoming a group from the Israelites' experience of becoming a people?

Evidence of Understanding

- Students will learn the Hebrew name of the Book of Exodus, *Sh'mot*.

- Students will freely, and with understanding, use the term *"parashah"* in conversation.

- Students will articulate that the Book of Exodus is made up of many *parshiyot*.

- Students will be able to draw a connection between their understanding of what it means to become a group and the experience of the Israelites in the Book of Exodus.

New Vocabulary

b'rachah	Hebrew word for "blessing," "prayer"
parashah (pl. *parshiyot*)	Torah portion of the week

Materials Needed

- One *Chumash*, or Bible, for each student (see introductory activity)

- Colored index cards (one color for each group)

ACTIVITY PLAN

I. INTRODUCTION TO THE FIVE BOOKS OF MOSES

Goals

- To enable students to situate the Book of *Sh'mot* in the Torah, helping them determine that there are five books in the Torah and that *Sh'mot* is the second one.

- To demonstrate that each book of the Torah has an English and a Hebrew name, and to introduce students to the English and Hebrew name of the second book of the Torah.

Provide a copy of the Torah for each student or groups of up to three students.

NOTE: The teacher may choose from the following editions of the Torah: *The Torah: A Modern Commentary* (New York: UAHC Press, 1981); *The Torah: The Five Books of Moses* (Philadelphia, PA: The Jewish Publication Society, 1962); *Tanakh: The Holy Scriptures* (Philadelphia, PA: The Jewish Publication Society, 1985); and *The Five Books of Moses*, The Schocken Bible: Volume I, translation and commentaries by Everett Fox (New York: Schocken Books, 1995) (English text only).

Learning Activities: Torah Search

1. Hand out copies of the Torah.

2. Break students into groups of up to three people.

3. Point out where the name of the book can be found on a given page of the Torah text (for example, in the JPS *Tanakh*, the name of the book is always in the upper left-hand corner, or right-hand corner, depending on whether the opening follows the English or Hebrew direction).

4. Ask students to leaf through the Torah and try to find the names of as many books as they can. If a full Bible (*Tanach*) is used, mark where the Torah ends so the students only search in the Torah section of the Bible (see attached activity worksheet). (5 minutes)

5. While students are working, post the cards with the names of each book of the Torah (in English, Hebrew, and transliteration) at the front of the room. The cards, five in all, can be found at the end of this lesson (pp. 24–25).

6. At the end of the activity, ask each group to write on the board one of the names it was able to find. After all the groups have written names, the teacher (or the students) can match the names the students came up with to the cards hung at the front of the room.

Summary of Activity

- Point out that every Torah scroll in the world is made up of these five books. Point out their names in Hebrew and in English (students are not expected to memorize these names).

- Indicate that the class will be studying parts of the second book of the Torah (ask students to name it) during the next several weeks.

II.   INTRODUCTION TO THE BOOK OF *SH'MOT*

Goals

- To familiarize students with the concept of *parashah* and the specific *parshiyot* of the Book of *Sh'mot*

- To introduce a major theme of the book: The Israelites become a people

- To demonstrate that each *parashah* focuses on a particular aspect of becoming a people

- To demonstrate to students that becoming a people is similar to becoming a group or a class (of students)

Learning Activities

Set Induction: Becoming a Group—Students' Experiences

1. Break students into groups of four or five people and give each group ten colored index cards (they can be white, but color is more fun).

2. Ask students to think of a group they are part of and in which they feel comfortable (e.g., a class, group at camp, group of friends).

3. Ask students to think about how they felt at first when they became part of the group, and to think about what it feels like now to be part of that same group.

4. Ask the students (within the small groups) to discuss and write down the answers to the following question (which the teacher should have written on the board beforehand): What are the stages (or steps) that you and other members of the group (class, friends) went through to become a group (for example, learning each other's names, learning who likes what, or getting through difficult moments together)? [One answer per index card] (10 minutes)

   NOTE: If students have trouble writing the answers on index cards, at the end of the activity they can tell the teacher and she or he can write for them (or a teacher's assistant can help them during the discussion).

5. Ask a student from each group to bring you the cards, in the correct order, once the activity is completed. Tape them on a wall or board.

Summary of Activity

- As they finish, ask a student from each group to tape the group's cards on the board or on a wall in order of stages.

Becoming a People (Group)

1. Hang up, in order of *parashah*, the cards attached to this unit.

2. Ask students to come close to the wall where their cards and the *parashah* cards are hung.

3. Have students answer the following questions: Thinking about the stages (or steps) of becoming a group as illustrated by your cards and looking at the cards of the Book of *Sh'mot*, what is similar and what is different between them? What items from the *Sh'mot* list could be added to our own list?

4. Ask students to sit, either in a circle on the floor in front of where the cards are hanging or at their desks.

Method

- Explain that each stage/card is one *parashah* or section of the Book of *Sh'mot*. Each section is made up of one or several stories and/or rules and laws. Ask students to name a few of the *parshiyot* that they see on the cards, to read the description out loud to the group (with the teacher's help, if necessary), and to try to guess what the stories or rules in the *parashah* might be about (this is to check their understanding that each card represents a *parashah* and that each *parashah* is made up of stories and/or rules/laws). An example from *Parashat Mishpatim*: God tells the Israelites not to hurt each other and to take care of each other.

- Point out that all the *parshiyot* in the Book of *Sh'mot*, when put together, tell the story of the Israelites becoming a group: the Jewish people.

- Note that just like it takes time for us to be a group, it took a lot of time for the Israelites, who were slaves in Egypt, to become a people.

- Explain that during the next few weeks the class will be looking at the ups and downs of becoming one Jewish people as told in the *parshiyot* of the Book of *Sh'mot*.

- Ask students which *parashah*, according to the topics listed on the cards, seems most interesting to them and about which they might like to learn more.

Homework

Students should talk with their parent(s) about the following questions, and write down their responses in the space provided in their TORAH JOURNAL.

1. What is the best part of being a member of a group?

2. What is the hardest part of being a member of a group?

Book Cards

בְּרֵאשִׁית

B'reishit

Genesis

שְׁמוֹת

Sh'mot

Exodus

וַיִּקְרָא

Vayikra

Leviticus

בְּמִדְבַּר

B'midbar
Numbers

דְּבָרִים

D'varim
Deuteronomy

The Five Books of Torah

Instructions

1. As you look through the Torah, focus on the very top of the page, where you will find the names of the five books of the Torah.
2. As you find them, copy them onto the lines below. Don't worry about being able to pronounce them. Just copy them as you see them.

Book 1:_____

Book 2:_____

Book 3:_____

Book 4:_____

Book 5:_____

Parashah Cards

Cut out the cards below and hang them on the wall.

Parashat Sh'mot

Parashat Va-eira

Parashat Bo

Parashat B'shalach

Parashat Yitro

Parashat Mishpatim

God sees the Israelites are in trouble and decides to bring them out of slavery.

Moses, who has agreed to lead the Israelites out of Egypt, tries to convince Pharaoh, the king of Egypt, to let them go. No success.

Moses is still trying to convince Pharaoh. The Israelites are told about a special sign that will mark them as a group and which they should put on their doors. God will skip over houses with that special sign.

Ups and downs: The Israelites leave Egypt. A big miracle happens and the Israelites are feeling special. But they are also scared about leaving their homes in Egypt, and going to a new place.

Moses, the Jews' leader, doesn't know how to run the group of Israelites. Yitro, his father-in-law, helps him figure out what to do.

God gives the Israelites rules for managing together and Moses tells them the rules.

Parashat T'rumah

Parashat T'tzaveh

Parashat Ki Tisa

Parashat Vayak'heil

Parashat P'kudei

The Israelites figure out how to make a place to store the rules so they'll be remembered and kept safe.

Rules telling the best way to thank God for all that's been done and to remember what God did to help the Israelites.

Ups and downs: The Israelites get scared and forget the rules. Moses convinces God to forgive the Israelites and give them the rules again.

Everyone works together to build a place to store the rules and remember God.

The Israelites figure out how to take God with them wherever they go.

Parashat Sh'mot: Finding God in Small Places

Introduction: Lesson Overview

This lesson is based on two texts. One is taken from the first Torah portion (*parashah*) of the Book of Exodus (*Sh'mot*). The second text is a commentary on *Parashat Sh'mot,* which comes from a midrash (an interpretation of the biblical text). It is important to note that there are multiple interpretations of this biblical text, and that the midrash used here represents only one possible interpretation. This commentary has been chosen for its ability to help students bring the biblical text into their world in a very concrete way.

The final piece of the lesson introduces the students to those blessings that can be recited daily, regardless of where or at what time. The goal is to help students recognize that there are many things, moments, and places which although seemingly ordinary or unworthy of any notice, are, upon reflection, really quite extraordinary and deserving of blessing.

Enduring understanding

➤ Torah is an ongoing dialogue between the text and its students.

➤ Torah is real in our daily lives; it is with us wherever we are.

➤ Developing the skills to study Torah is essential to integrating Torah into our lives.

Essential Questions

1. What does the Torah have to say to me and to my world?

2. Why is the Torah different from other books?

3. How can Torah study help me in my everyday life?

Questions to be Addressed

• Why did God appear to Moses in a thorn bush?

• How long did it take Moses to notice (realize) that the bush wasn't burning up and that there was something special about that bush?

• What are the implications of stopping and focusing to "see" God in the world?

• What is the value of seemingly lowly or ugly things in our world?

• Where do we find God?

Evidence of Understanding

• Students are able to explain the reason why, according to the midrash used for this lesson, God appeared to Moses in a thorn bush.

• Students are able to relate a story of a time in their lives when they discovered something beautiful or godly in a place where they didn't think it possible to happen.

• Students are able to describe an experience of gradual realization, when something seemingly ugly turned out to be holy and special.

• Students are able determine which blessing to recite upon seeing certain seemingly ordinary things.

New Vocabulary

midrash

The term *midrash* (pl. *midrashim*) refers to written interpretations of biblical texts. Midrash can refer to a specific book of midrashim, the most well known of which is Midrash *Rabbah,* written during the rabbinic period, or it can be used as a generic term referring to any interpretation of a biblical text. There are both ancient and modern midrashim.

tikkun olam

This term means "repairing (*tikkun*) of the world (*olam*)." The concept of *tikkun olam* is based on the interpretation Jewish mysticism gave to the story of creation. According to the mystical interpretation, there are sparks of God's light scattered in vessels throughout the world waiting to be reunited with their source (God). Every time we perform a mitzvah and make the world a better place, we send one of these pieces of godly light back to the Infinite One (God).

The Text

NOTE: The following is from *The Torah: A Modern Commentary*, W. G. Plaut ed. (New York: UAHC Press, 1981), and is meant for the teacher only. The biblical text provided for the students on p. 39—based on this same version—has been modified and simplified in order to facilitate the class' understanding of the story.

1] Now Moses, tending the flock of his father-in-law Jethro, the priest of Midian, drove the flock into the wilderness, and came to Horeb, the mountain of God. 2] An angel of the LORD appeared to him in a blazing fire out of a bush. He gazed, and there was a bush all aflame, yet the bush was not consumed. 3] Moses said, "I must turn aside to look at this marvelous sight; why doesn't the bush burn up?" 4] When the LORD saw that he had turned aside to look, God called to him out of the bush: "Moses! Moses!" He answered, "Here I am." 5] And He said, "Do not come closer. Remove your sandals from your feet, for the place on which you stand is holy ground. 6] I am," He said, "the God of your father, the God of Abraham, the God of Isaac, and the God of Jacob." And Moses hid his face, for he was afraid to look at God.

Exodus 3:1–6

MIDRASH

Someone once asked a rabbi: "Why did God choose to appear in a bush?" He answered, "Had God appeared in a carob tree or a sycamore, you would have asked the same question. However, it would be wrong to let you go without a reply, so I will tell you why it was a bush: to teach you that no place is devoid of God's presence, not even a lowly bush."

Exodus *Rabbah* 2:5

ACTIVITY PLAN

I. SET INDUCTION

Goal

- To introduce students to the notion that what they think they see may not be what they are really seeing, and that sometimes it takes time to figure out what is really in front of us. This exercise precedes the introduction of the story of Moses, who has to stop and *gaze* at the bush for a while in order to see that it is not burning up—as one would normally expect.

Materials

- magnifying glass

- a collection of ordinary objects such as a leaf, a book, a stone, etc.

- a picture of an optical illusion

Activity

- Using a picture of an optical illusion, ask students to write on a piece of paper, in three words or less, what they see.

- Ask them to look at the picture a second time, trying to see something else. If they see a different image, they should write down on a piece of paper, in three words or less, what they see.

Questions for Discussion

- What did you see the first time you looked?

- Did you see something different the second time you looked? If so, what?

- How long did it take you to notice the different images in the picture?

II. TEXT STUDY

Goal

- To help students draw a parallel between their experience in the first activity of this lesson and the text from the Book of Exodus. In particular, students should focus on how long or how many times Moses had to look at the bush to realize what was happening before him was very unusual.

Activity

- Hand out copies of the text to each student. (See p. 39).

- Read the text aloud. The teacher can dramatically read the text, semi-acting it out. If there are one or more students who are good readers, they can read and act the text out.

Class Discussion

1. Ask students to recount the text, to ensure that they have an understanding of the storyline. This should be brief and to the point.

2. Looking at verse 2, ask them to answer the following: How long do you think Moses looked at the bush before he realized it wasn't burning up?

3. What does this have to do with the first part of this lesson, when you looked at the picture?

4. A long time ago, according to a midrash, a person asked a rabbi: "Why did God choose to appear in a bush?" With a partner, try to come up with an answer to the person's question.

5. Ask the pairs to report their answers. Write them on the board.

6. After the students discuss this question and try to take a guess at what the rabbi's answer might have been, read aloud to them Midrash Exodus *Rabbah* 2:5.

III. God in Lowly Places

Goal

- To enable students to see the extraordinary in the seemingly ordinary

Activity

- This is a detective activity in which students are asked to closely examine a mundane object and find what is amazing about it— to find God's imprint.

- Divide students into pairs.

- Distribute one object to each pair. Objects should be typical objects that one encounters every day. They might include a rock, a leaf or flower, a book, a pencil, a pen, a can opener, a computer floppy disk, etc.

- If possible, make several magnifying glasses available.

- Ask students to examine the object very closely, and in so doing to keep in mind the following guidelines:

  1. Describe this object.

  2. What is it made of? (If it applies to the given object: What holds its parts together?)

  3. What is it used for?

  4. Could you say that there is some "magic" in this object? What is it? [The teacher should explain this question by giving an example. For instance, a "pencil": an ordinary, everyday object whose magic resides in the fact that it comes from a tree, and that a tree grows up thanks to water, that the water comes from the sky in the form of rain and feeds animals and plants that in turn help us—human beings—stay alive as well. When we think of this long life-process we realize that a simple pencil becomes a "special" thing, full of life and a "history" of its own.]

- Reconvene students and ask them to report back: What was hard to explain about your object? What questions did you find harder to answer? What is "magical" about the object?

What Does This All Mean?

- At this point, the teacher should help students understand the main lesson to be drawn by these exercises: Even in the simplest, most common objects, there is something special, worthy of our attention, "magic." Perhaps that is where God is or the part God plays in making things function and exist.

IV.   MYSTICAL CREATION STORY
Goal

- To emphasize the concept that God resides in lowly as well as exalted places in the world.

- To start students on the never-ending search for God in all things.

Activity

NOTE: If time is short, skip this section and move directly to "Discussion Wrap Up."

- Read aloud the "Mystical Creation Story." (See pp. 40–41.)

- After the reading, ask students the following:

  According to this story: Where do we find God? Who can find/see God?

Discussion Wrap-Up

God is in all things, even common or ugly things. Our job as human beings and Jews is to find the traces (or "pieces") of God in the world. Judaism is so focused on seeing God in everything that it has many blessings so we can bless everything we see or do.

Hand out copies of the blessings (pp. 42–43), noting that blessings are the way Jews acknowledge having noticed the godliness of something they see or experience.

Blessings

❖ Blessing on seeing lightning

❖ Blessing on hearing thunder

❖ Blessing on seeing a rainbow

❖ Blessing for natural beauty (in things, wildlife, or people)

❖ Blessing for unusual people or animals

❖ Blessing for seeing the first seasonal blossom of the trees

   • Review the blessings with the students, making sure they can read them.

   • If there is time, ask which blessings the students 1) find funny, 2) like, 3) want to recite right away

   • Time permitting, students might want to say the first six words in Hebrew and the last part of the blessing in English. The teacher can practice this with the students.

Homework

Moses was able to see God in a little thorn bush and, because he stopped and noticed God in the bush, God was able to ask him to free the Israelites from Egypt. If Moses hadn't stopped long enough to really look at the bush and to finally notice that it wasn't burning up, he would have not heard God and freed the Israelites and we, the Jews, would not be here today as a free people.

   1. During the next week, it's your turn to be like Moses and notice God in all kinds of places. Try to notice one or two things over which you can say a blessing. In particular try to notice something special about what you do every day. You might want to take your blessing sheet with you when you go shopping with a parent or on a walk together, and see if you notice

something that you (and your parent) want to say a blessing over. Remember, the thing you want to thank God for doesn't have to be especially beautiful or big. It should be something you notice that you don't usually notice. If you don't have your blessing sheet with you, make up your own blessing!

2. In your TORAH JOURNAL, write what you blessed and which blessing you used. Give a short description of what you saw that was godly and special, and what the "uniqueness," "magic" of this object was.

THE TEXT

1] Now Moses, while taking care of the flock of his father-in-law Jethro, the priest of Midian, drove the flock into the wilderness and came to Horeb, the mountain of God.

2] An angel of *Adonai* appeared to him in a blazing fire out of a bush. He gazed, and there was a burning bush, yet the bush was not consumed (eaten up).

3] Moses said, "I must turn aside to look at this amazing sight; why doesn't the bush burn up?"

4] When *Adonai* saw that he had stopped to look, God called to him out of the bush: "Moses, Moses!" He answered, "Here I am." 5] And God said, "Do not come closer. Remove your sandals from your feet, for the place where you are standing is holy ground.

6] I am," God said, "the God of your father, the God of Abraham, the God of Isaac, and the God of Jacob." And Moses hid his face, for he was afraid to look at God.

Exodus 3:1–6

MIDRASH

Someone once asked a rabbi: "Why did God choose to appear in a bush?" He answered, "Had God appeared in a carob tree or a sycamore, you would have asked the same question. However, it would be wrong to let you go without a reply, so I will tell you why it was a bush: to teach you that no place is without God's presence, not even a lowly bush."

Exodus *Rabbah* 2:5

THE MYSTICAL CREATION STORY

A long, long time ago God decided to create the world. God looked around for a good place to put the world, but couldn't find it. Why? Well, because there was no free space in the universe. Don't you remember? God is everywhere!

Now, think about this: If God takes up all the space in the endless universe, then *where* could God place this newest creation—our world? God was so great to think to create us, but had nowhere to "put" us. What to do? As always, God found a solution to this problem: God "shrank"! Well, perhaps "contracted" is a better word for what God did. Imagine God pulling in a deep breath (like when we suck in our stomachs) in order to pull in a little and "empty" the necessary space in which to place the world. How amazing! Only God could come up with such a brilliant idea—to give up a bit of God's never-ending universe to make space for us! For hundreds and hundreds of years, Jews have called this awesome event the *tzimtzum*. So now if someone asks you what *tzimtzum* is, you will know: It is the process by which God contracted ("shrank"!) to make room for the world.

After God made enough room and the world was created, the world had to be filled with God's light. By the word "light" we mean much more than simply "light": in God's light there is God's love, spirit, beauty, and lots of awesome, good things. So God had to find a way to fill the world with this light. Another great idea came to God's mind. God decided to use giant pots as containers for the light, and from these "vessels of light," set up above the world, God's presence beamed down and filled up God's creation.

At first this idea seemed to work really well. But, then something terrible happened. God's divine light was too intense and powerful for the pots to hold. The containers cracked! Millions and millions of godly light-sparks were released in the universe and scattered all over the world. As you can imagine, every single tiniest inch of God's light is a priceless treasure!

God managed to get some of the light back before it got to Earth. But not everything was recovered. Some sparks of light still lie unseen in our world.

How can we find these sparks? Well, it's up to us: we must look really carefully at all of God's creation to be able to spot God's beauty and presence—God's light—in them. You never know where you can run into a spark of God's light! It could be anywhere. A flower, a funny-looking rock, a warm loaf of bread or a fellow human being might all contain within themselves sparks of God. And the beauty of it all is that God wants us to help recover those sparks and send them back to God. Every time we do a mitzvah (God's commandments), every time we act righteously, we return one of those sparks to their source—to God.

But if it's so hard to find the scattered fragments of God's light, why should we bother? Because, when all the sparks were together, neatly gathered under God's control in the giant pots, the world was perfect. But since that disaster—the explosion of the pots, and the mess that followed it—the world is full of problems: pain, unhappiness, and injustice. If we all want the world to be perfect again, then we must keep looking for those sparks, and help God recover all of God's wonderful pieces of light. When we notice one, the spark goes (whoosh!) right back to God.

Someone who really paid attention to traces of God on earth was Moses. When he saw the burning bush, Moses didn't just keep going: he realized that there was something fabulous going on and that this wonder should not be ignored. He was right, because as we know from the Torah, God was in that burning bush.

Like Moses, when we spot a spark of God's light in the world and when we do a mitzvah, we help God rebuild the broken pots. There is a name for this, too: it's called "*tikkun olam*" which is the Hebrew way of saying "repairing the world."

Are you interested in repairing the world? Then look for your next spark of God's light!

Blessings for Daily Life

Upon seeing lightning

Blessed are You, *Adonai*, our God, Ruler of the universe,
Who makes the work of creation.

בָּרוּךְ אַתָּה יְיָ אֱלֹהֵינוּ מֶלֶךְ הָעוֹלָם, עֹשֶׂה מַעֲשֵׂה בְרֵאשִׁית.

Upon hearing thunder

Blessed are You, *Adonai*, our God, Ruler of the universe,
Whose strength and power fill the universe.

בָּרוּךְ אַתָּה יְיָ אֱלֹהֵינוּ מֶלֶךְ הָעוֹלָם, שֶׁכֹּחוֹ וּגְבוּרָתוֹ מָלֵא עוֹלָם.

Upon seeing a rainbow

Blessed are You, *Adonai*, our God, Ruler of the universe,
for You remember the covenant, You are faithful to
Your covenant and You fulfill Your word.

בָּרוּךְ אַתָּה יְיָ אֱלֹהֵינוּ מֶלֶךְ הָעוֹלָם, זוֹכֵר הַבְּרִית וְנֶאֱמָן בִּבְרִיתוֹ
וְקַיָּם בְּמַאֲמָרוֹ.

Upon admiring natural beauty (of things, wildlife, or people)

Blessed are You, *Adonai*, our God, Ruler of the universe,
Whose world is filled with such beauty.

בָּרוּךְ אַתָּה יְיָ אֱלֹהֵינוּ מֶלֶךְ הָעוֹלָם, שֶׁכָּכָה לוֹ בְּעוֹלָמוֹ.

Upon seeing unusual
people or animals

Blessed are You, *Adonai*, our God, Ruler of the universe,
Who makes creatures different.

בָּרוּךְ אַתָּה יְיָ אֱלֹהֵינוּ מֶלֶךְ הָעוֹלָם, מְשַׁנֶּה הַבְּרִיּוֹת.

Upon seeing the first seasonal
blossom of the trees

Blessed are You, *Adonai*, our God, Ruler of the universe,
for You have made in Your universe good creatures
and good trees in which to please humankind.

בָּרוּךְ אַתָּה יְיָ אֱלֹהֵינוּ מֶלֶךְ הָעוֹלָם, אֲשֶׁר בָּרָא בְּעוֹלָמוֹ בְּרִיּוֹת
טוֹבוֹת וְאִלָנוֹת טוֹבִים, לְהַנּוֹת בָּהֶם בְּנֵי אָדָם.

Parashat Bo: Marking Our Freedom

Introduction: Lesson Overview

The lesson on *Parashat Bo* is divided into two sessions. The first session (א, Alef) will focus on the text from the Book of Exodus which describes the Israelites marking their doorposts on the night of the Exodus. The parallel will then be drawn between the Israelites' actions and the use of a mezuzah (pl. mezuzot) on the doorposts of Jewish homes. Using the *V'ahavta* prayer, which is inserted and kept inside the mezuzah, students will begin to think about actions that are special and remind them of God and their Jewishness. The second session (ב, Bet) will be devoted to having students create their own mezuzah and learn the rituals for affixing it. Teachers may choose to divide up the unit differently by doing the last part of the first session (the *V'ahavta* worksheet) at the beginning of the second session. In either case, be sure to remind students of what happened in the previous session.

This lesson is based on Exodus 12:1, 3–7, 11–14a: God commands the Israelites to mark the doorposts of their houses with lamb's blood so that they will be passed over (skipped) by the tenth plague—the killing of all Egyptian first-born.

NOTE: Although it is written that the Jews were commanded to mark their doors with lamb's blood, this lesson avoids using the exact biblical terminology. For the purpose of introducing young children to the story of the Exodus, "blood" has been replaced by the terms "marking," "markers," or "signs."

Enduring Understanding

➤ Torah is an ongoing dialogue between the text and its students.

➤ Torah is real in our daily lives; it is with us wherever we are.

➤ Developing the skills to study Torah is essential to integrating Torah into our lives.

Essential Questions

1. What does the Torah have to say to me and to my world?

2. Why is the Torah different from other books?

3. How can Torah study help me in my everyday life?

Questions to be Addressed

• Why did the Israelites mark the doorposts just before they left Egypt?

• Can you think of a way in which Jews still "mark" their doors to this day?

• Why do Jews today continue to mark their doors as the Israelites did in Egypt?

• Are there other symbols/marks you can think of that indicate that a certain house is a "Jewish house"? (Answers may include: a menorah, a seder plate, etc.)

Evidence of Understanding

• Students are able to articulate the connection between the Israelites' marking of their homes and the mezuzah used to mark Jewish homes today. (Session א)

• Students are able to articulate that the mezuzah—just like the marks on the doors of the Israelites—is a signal to remind us that we are free. (Session א)

• Students will have created a mezuzah, which reflects their understanding of what it means for them to be Jewish as expressed in the *V'ahavta*. (Sessions א and ב)

• Students will be able to recite the *b'rachah* (blessing) for affixing a mezuzah. (Session ב)

New Vocabulary

b'rachah (pl. *b'rachot*)	Jewish blessing; prayer
Exodus	Mass departure, emigration. "Exodus" is the name of the second book of the Torah, which describes the story of the mass emigration of the Israelites from the land of Egypt.
klaf (pl. *klafim*)	The piece of parchment inside a mezuzah, on which the *V'ahavta* prayer is written

mezuzah (pl. mezuzot)	The small box or holder (usually finely decorated), containing a parchment with a selection from the Torah, that is affixed on the doorpost of Jewish homes
V'ahavta	(*lit.* "And you shall love") First word of the prayer that commands the Jews to love God and that thanks God for delivering the Israelites out of the land of Egypt. The *V'ahavta* is inscribed on the piece of parchment (*klaf*) kept in the mezuzah box

The Text

NOTE: The following is from *The Torah: A Modern Commentary*, W. G. Plaut ed. (New York: UAHC Press, 1981), and is meant for the teacher only. The biblical text provided for the students on p. 53—based on this same version—has been modified and simplified in order to facilitate the class' understanding of story.

1] The LORD said to Moses and Aaron in the land of Egypt: … 3] Speak to the whole community of Israel and say that on the tenth of this month each of them shall take a lamb to a family, a lamb to a household. 4] But if the household is too small for a lamb, then let him share one with the neighbor closest to his household in the number of persons: you shall apportion the lamb according to what each person should eat. 5] Your lamb shall be without blemish, a yearling male; you may take it from the sheep or from the goats. 6] You shall keep watch over it until the fourteenth day of this month; and all the aggregate community of the Israelites shall slaughter it at twilight. 7] They shall take some of the blood and put it on the two doorposts and the lintel of the houses in which they are to eat it. 8] They shall eat the flesh that same night; they shall eat it roasted over the fire, with unleavened bread and with bitter herbs. 9] Do not eat any of it raw, or cooked in any way with water, but roasted—head, legs and entrails—over the fire. 10] You shall not leave any of it over until morning; if any of it is left until morning, you shall burn it.

11] This is how you shall eat it: your loins girded, your sandals on your feet, and your staff in your hand; and you shall eat it hurriedly: it is a passover offering to the LORD. 12] For that night I will go through the land of Egypt and strike down every first-born in the land of Egypt, both man and beast; and I will mete out punishments to all the gods of Egypt, I the LORD. 13] And the blood on the houses in which you dwell shall be a sign for you: when I see the blood I will pass over you, so that no plague will destroy you when I strike the land of Egypt.

14] This day shall be to you one of remembrance: you shall celebrate it as a festival to the LORD throughout the ages; you shall celebrate it as an institution for all time.

Exodus 12:1–14

ACTIVITY PLAN

I. SET INDUCTION

Goal

- To help students understand that we use symbols in order to remind ourselves of a particular thing every time we see them. For example, when I see snow I am reminded of winter, or when I see a menorah I think of Chanukah. This exercise is designed to introduce the concept of symbols as reminders. It will lead the way to teaching the interpretation that the markers on the doorposts of the Israelites in Egypt were a symbol of their soon-to-be-acquired freedom, just as the mezuzot on the doors of Jewish homes today are a reminder of freedom, our God, and Jewish obligations.

Learning Activity

Ask each student to orally fill in the following sentence:

When I see _____, I am reminded of/about_____.

Give an example: When I see snow, I am reminded of winter. The teacher should write the students' suggestions (snow = winter) on the board or on a flipchart page.

II. ISRAELITES MARKING THEIR FREEDOM: EXODUS 12:1–14
(15-20 minutes)

Goal

- To introduce students to this part the Book of Exodus

- To allow students to reflect on the reasons why the Israelites were asked to mark their doorways. This reflection will be guided by the interpretation given by Maimonides (Rabbi Moshe ben Maimon, also known as RaMBaM), according to which the marking was meant to remind the Israelites that they were about to go free. Maimonides' explanation differs from the common interpretation that sees the marking as a way of letting God know where the Jews lived in order to spare their first-born sons.

Activity

Tell students the story of the Exodus using the following as a guideline, and follow up with the comprehension questions. (It is important that the teacher actually tells the story—as opposed to reading it off the sheet—using gestures, facial expressions, and even props or actors that would make this story-telling come to life.)

THE STORY TELLING

Our ancestors, the Israelites, lived in Egypt. At the beginning they were treated well. After they had been living there for a long time, the Israelites were made into slaves because the pharaoh, the king of Egypt, was afraid that they were becoming too numerous and too strong. Pharaoh made life very difficult for the Israelites. They had to work from morning until night doing very hard physical work. The Israelites prayed to God to take them out of Egypt and make them free. God heard their prayers. God sent Moses to lead the Israelites out of Egypt, to freedom. Moses went to Pharaoh and said, "*Adonai*, the God of the Israelites says, 'Let my people go!' " Pharaoh did not know about *Adonai*, the God of the Israelites, and would not let his Jewish slaves go. So, God sent ten plagues down on the people of Egypt to show Pharaoh God's power and break his resistance. The plagues affected all the Egyptians, but did not hurt the Israelites. The first plague made the river (the central source of life for the country at that time) and all the waters in the fountains, pools, and canals of Egypt turn to blood; the second brought tons of frogs that covered all over the land; the third brought oodles of insects and the fourth hordes of wild animals that roamed the country and destroyed everything. The fifth plague was a terrible illness that killed cattle and all animals; the sixth consisted of boils from which neither man or beast remained immune and made all of Egypt agonize in pain. A terrible hail-storm followed and then a plague of grasshoppers that ate up everything they came across; the ninth plague made the world turn completely dark for three days. All the terrible things that were befalling the whole Egyptian nation did not touch or involve the place where the Israelites lived—they were spared from the plagues. It was an awfully tough time for the Egyptians. And yet Pharaoh would not let the Israelites go. God decided that it was time for the most difficult and serious punishment of all, the tenth plague: in one night God was going to kill all the first-born of Egypt—human and animal.

Comprehension Questions

1. Why did the Israelites want to leave Egypt?

2. Why couldn't the Israelites just pack their things and go? Who was keeping them from doing so?

3. How did God intervene in favor of the Jews?

4. At the point where we left off our story, what was about to happen?

Text Reading and Discussion

- Hand out copies of the biblical text to each students (p. 53) and read it aloud together with them.

- Discuss the following two questions, recording students' answers to question two on the board or on a flipchart page.

    Question 1:   What does God tell the Israelites to do?

    Question 2:   Verse 13 says that the marks on the houses is a sign for the Israelites. Think back to the sentence you filled in earlier when we began our lesson: "When I see a/an _____, I am reminded of/about_____" … How would the Israelites fill in this sentence: "When I see a <u>marker</u> on the side and top of the door of my house, I am reminded of/about _____."

- At the end of the discussion, point out that this question is open to various interpretations and that therefore practically every answer is correct. Also explain that one famous rabbi, Moshe ben Maimon (often referred to simply as Maimonides, or Rambam), thought that the marks were put on the doors to remind the Israelites that they were about to be set free.

- Ask if the students agree or disagree with Rambam's idea. Why or why not?

IV.   MAKING OUR SIGNS: MEZUZOT IN OUR LIVES
   (20–25 minutes)

Goal

- To draw a connection between the mezuzot on Jewish doorways/homes and the marks on the doors of the Israelite homes in Egypt on the night of the Exodus

- To introduce students to the object and symbolism of the mezuzah and its role as a Jewish marker in our homes

- To identify the acts mentioned in the *V'ahavta* and their connection to the mezuzah (which reminds us to follow God's "instructions" contained in the *V'ahavta*)

A. Introduction to the Mezuzah

- Just as the Israelites marked their doors, we mark our doors with a special object today to remind ourselves about freedom.

- Ask students if they know what those markers are called.

- If possible, take a walk around the synagogue looking for mezuzot. Ask students to notice what is on each mezuzah. What do the different shapes and designs of the mezuzot symbolize?

    NOTE: The teacher can help the students understand this question by pointing out that mezuzot come in a large variety of shapes, colors, sizes, and so on. A mezuzah in the shape of a scroll reminds us of Torah and Torah study, for example; other mezuzot represent Jerusalem to remind us of Israel, etc. But no matter what the design of a mezuzah, all mezuzot remind us of our freedom, and all mezuzot contain the same prayer.

- If classes take place in a non-Jewish building, ask students to describe mezuzot they have seen or, if possible, bring in examples or pictures of different mezuzot. What do they think the designs of these mezuzot are trying to remind them of?

B. Inside a Mezuzah

- Bring a *klaf* to class. If an original one is too hard to find, you can cut out the *klaf* at the end of this unit (see p. 62).

- Ask whether the students know what is inside a mezuzah and what is written on the *klaf*'s parchment. Show them the *klaf*.

- Hand out a photocopy of the *klaf* with the *V'ahavta* and its English translation.

- Read the *V'ahavta* aloud (or ask the students to do so).

- Ask if students have heard the prayer before or know it.

- What do they think it is about?

- Divide students into groups of three or four and instruct them to do the following activity, using the *V'ahavta* worksheet at the end of this unit:

    NOTE: Instead of the eleven choices offered in the worksheet, teachers may want to narrow the choices to three or five.

    1. Pick two of the ways the *V'ahavta* tells us to remember God.

    2. Answer the questions on the ways to remind ourselves of God that follow each quote from the *V'ahavta*.

    3. On a blank sheet, illustrate or write the answers to your questions.

        - Ask each group to present one of its answers.

- As groups finish the activity, the teacher should take all answer sheets, which will later be placed in a class mezuzah.

- Point out that everyone's way of remembering God will be part of the class mezuzah.

Homework

Many Jews place a mezuzah on the front door of their house and on the doorway to every room in their home (except for the bathrooms). When walking into each room, the mezuzah is a reminder that God is in that room (in every room) and that the room is special, just as the marks on the door of Israelite homes in Egypt indicated that the Israelites were about to go free and reminded God not to harm the people in the marked homes.

With a parent, discuss the following questions and write down your answers:

1. On the door of which room in your house would you like to place a mezuzah?

2. What is special about the room that you would like to remember each time you enter it?

3. What other special things would you like to be reminded of as you walk into that room?

NOTE TO PARENTS: Your child will be asked to use the answers to these questions in the creation of his or her very own mezuzah for the room he or she has chosen.

A passover offering to God...

THE BIBLICAL TEXT

1] *Adonai* said to Moses and Aaron in the land of Egypt [...]

3] Speak to the whole community of Israel and say that on the tenth of this month each family and household will take a lamb.

4] But if the household is too small for a lamb, let him share one with a neighbor who lives nearby [...]

5] Your lamb should have no marks[1] [...]

7] The Israelites shall take some of the blood and put it on the two sides and top of the door of the houses where they are going to eat it [...]

11] [...] it is a passover offering to the LORD.

12] For on that night I will go through the land of Egypt, and strike down every firstborn in the land of Egypt, both human and animal; and I will give out punishments to all the gods of Egypt, I *Adonai*.

13] And the blood on the houses where you are staying will be a sign for you: when I see this mark I will pass over you, so that no plague will destroy you.

14: This day shall be to you a day to remember: you will celebrate it as a festival to *Adonai* throughout time; you will celebrate it as a marker for all time.

Exodus 12:1–14

---

[1] It should be perfect

ואהבת

V'ahavta

V'ahavta et Adonai Elohecha, b'chol l'vav'cha uv'chol naf'sh'cha uv'chol m'odecha.

V'hayu had'varim ha'eileh asher anochi m'tzav'cha hayom al l'vavecha.

V'shinantam l'vanecha v'dibarta bam, b'shiv't'cha b'veitecha uv'lecht'cha vaderech uv'shoch'b'cha uv'kumecha. Uk'shartam l'ot al yadecha v'hayu l'totafot bein einecha.

Uch'tav'tam al m'zuzot beitecha uvish'arecha.

L'ma'an tizk'ru va'asitem et kol mitz'votai v'hiyitem k'doshim leiloheichem. Ani Adonai Eloheichem asher hotzeiti et'chem me'eretz Mitz'rayim lih'yot lachem leilohim. Ani Adonai Eloheichem.

You shall love the Lord your God with all your mind, with all your strength, with all your being.

Set these words, which I command you this day, upon your heart. Teach them faithfully to your children; speak of them in your home and on your way, when you lie down and when you rise up.

Bind them as a sign upon your hand; let them be a symbol before your eyes; inscribe them on the doorposts of your house, and on your gates.

Be mindful of all My mitzvot, and do them: so shall you consecrate yourselves to your God. I, the Lord, am your God who led you out of Egypt to be your God; I, the Lord, am your God.

Deuteronomy 6:4-9, Numbers 15:40-41

שְׁמַע יִשְׂרָאֵל יְהֹוָה אֱלֹהֵינוּ יְהֹוָה אֶחָד: וְאָהַבְתָּ אֵת יְהֹוָה אֱלֹהֶיךָ
בְּכָל־לְבָבְךָ, וּבְכָל־נַפְשְׁךָ, וּבְכָל־מְאֹדֶךָ: וְהָיוּ הַדְּבָרִים הָאֵלֶּה אֲשֶׁר
אָנֹכִי מְצַוְּךָ הַיּוֹם עַל־לְבָבֶךָ: וְשִׁנַּנְתָּם לְבָנֶיךָ וְדִבַּרְתָּ בָּם בְּשִׁבְתְּךָ
בְּבֵיתֶךָ וּבְלֶכְתְּךָ בַדֶּרֶךְ וּבְשָׁכְבְּךָ וּבְקוּמֶךָ: וּקְשַׁרְתָּם לְאוֹת עַל־יָדֶךָ
וְהָיוּ לְטֹטָפֹת בֵּין עֵינֶיךָ: וּכְתַבְתָּם עַל־מְזֻזֹת בֵּיתֶךָ וּבִשְׁעָרֶיךָ:

V'ahavta Worksheet

And you shall love the Lord your God with your whole heart...

1. Question: How do you love God with your heart?

_____

_____

...and with your whole soul...

2. Question: When do you feel God in your soul?

_____

_____

...and with all your might.

3. Question: When do you feel strong?

_____

_____

And these words, which I command you this day, will be in your heart; And you will always teach them to your children,

4. Question: How can you teach God's words (or what is right)?

_____

_____

And will talk of them when you sit in your house ...

5. Question: Think of a time when you had a very special conversation at home (with your mother, father, or siblings) that made you feel very good and taught you something important. Write it here.

_____

_____

...And when you walk outside...

6. Question: Where do you feel or sense God when you are out of your house?

_____

_____

...And when you lie down at night...

7. Question: What are you thankful for at the end of the day, and how do you remember to be thankful before you go to bed?

_____

_____

...And when you get up in the morning.

8. Question: What are you thankful for when you wake up in the morning?

_____

_____

...You will put them on your hands as a sign...

9. Question: Is there anything that you wear, or can wear, that would make you feel closer to God? Something that, when it is on your body, can be considered a symbol of your connection to God and Judaism?

_____

_____

...And they will be as frontlets between your eyes.

10. Question: Is there a particular time during the year, or a particular place you can think of, when God's presence is felt stronger than usual?

_____

_____

And you will write them on the doorposts of your house, and on your gates.

11. Question: What is your favorite mezuzah and why is it your favorite?

_____

_____

Parashat Bo: Marking Our Freedom

Introduction: Lesson overview

The goal of this session of the *Parashat Bo* lesson is to take the concept of mezuzah and bring it into the students' lives in a very personal way. They will have the opportunity to think of special memories or things that are worth thanking God for. As a reminder/symbol of these things, students will create a mezuzah to bring home and post on the door of a room.

This lesson is based on Exodus 12:1, 3–7, 11–14: God commands the Israelites to mark the doorposts of their houses so they will be passed over (skipped) by the tenth plague—the killing of all Egyptian first-born.

Enduring understanding

➤ Torah is an ongoing dialogue between the text and its students.

➤ Torah is real in our daily lives; it is with us wherever we are.

➤ Developing the skills to study Torah is essential to integrating Torah into our lives.

Essential questions

1. What does the Torah have to say to me and to my world?

2. Why is the Torah different from other books?

3. How can Torah study help me in my everyday life?

Questions to be addressed

- Why did the Israelites mark their doorposts just before they left Egypt? (Session א)

- Can you think of a way in which Jews still "mark" their doors even today? (Session א)

- Why do Jews today continue to mark their doors as the Israelites did in Egypt? (Session א)

- How do you "mark" your home Jewishly? (Session א and ב)

Evidence of Understanding

- Students are able to articulate the connection between the Israelites' marking of the homes and the mezuzah used to mark Jewish homes today. (Session א)

- Students are able to articulate that the mezuzah—just like the marks on the doors of the Israelites—is a symbol to remind us that we are free. (Session א)

- Students will have created a mezuzah, which reflects their understanding of what it means for them to be free as expressed in the *V'ahavta*. (Sessions א and ב)

- Students will be able to recite the *b'rachah* for affixing a mezuzah. (Session ב)

Materials needed

For set induction:

- A shadow box (diorama)

- Transparent contact paper

- Double-sided tape for hanging the mezuzah

For mezuzah making:

- Two pieces of transparent Lucite/plastic with holes at the top and bottom, which line up (size: 7" x 3.5"). The Lucite can be ordered from most craft supply stores.

- Interesting wrapping paper, wallpaper scraps, magazines to be cut up, pictures of places and things (Jewish and otherwise), other interesting types of paper, scraps of ribbon, yarn, glitter shapes

- Glue

- Pieces of colored ribbon that will wrap lengthwise around both pieces of plastic (these will be used to bind the two pieces of plastic together)

- 3" x 3" paper with the *V'ahavta* printed on it. These may be purchased from any Judaica store. For the purpose of this project, it is possible to purchase a non-kosher *klaf* (which is very inexpensive), simply create your own, or photocopy the one provided at the end of this lesson (p. 62).

ACTIVITY PLAN

I.   Set Induction
(5–10 minutes)

Goal

- To remind students of the connection they made in the previous session between the use of the mezuzah in Jewish homes today as a reminder of God's presence and of our acquired freedom, and the way in which the Israelites marked their homes as a signal that they were about to be set free and led out of Egypt.

- To model the creation and affixing of a mezuzah

Learning Activity

1. Hand out the answer sheets from the *V'ahavta* activity from the previous session.

2. Point out that these sheets will now become the scrolls to be inserted inside your class mezuzah.

3. Introduce the students to the special mezuzah box that will become the class mezuzah.

4. Gather the students around the box. Ask them to pretend that they are in Egypt, and God is about to help them get free. What are they thinking about as they mark their doors so God will know to let them go?

5. Ask students to place their scrolls in the mezuzah box one by one, and tell them to describe one thing they were thinking about as they were pretending to be the Israelites in Egypt. When all students have placed their scroll in the box, place the transparent contact paper across the top.

6. Go over the *b'rachah* for affixing a mezuzah (written beforehand on the board). (See *b'rachah* sheet, p. 62)

7. Place the mezuzah in its permanent place in the classroom (can be on a table by the door, hung beside the door in the hall—depending on the ability to affix something permanently in the building)—and all recite the *b'rachah* as the mezuzah is placed.

II. MAKING MY SPECIAL MARKER
(35-40 minutes)

Goal

- Using the answers to the previous week's homework, students will design a mezuzah for a room in their house that will remind them of something special each time they walk in that room. The mezuzah should include some representation of what they want to remember. (Parents may be invited in to do this activity with the children.)

Instructions for Creating a Mezuzah

1. Ask students to think about what they want their mezuzah to represent.

2. To help students figure this out, remind them to think back to the answers to their homework from the previous session (א) on which they worked with their parents; and what they thought about when they were pretending to be the Israelites leaving Egypt.

3. Students should choose a piece of background paper from the wrapping paper, wallpaper, or any other image they choose (perhaps from a magazine or other interesting source).

4. Over this background paper, students can glue other items or pictures that will serve as reminders each time they see their mezuzah of what they have chosen to depict. Room should be left for the *klaf* with the *V'ahavta* that will have to be glued on the paper, too.

5. Once the glue has sufficiently dried, place the second piece of plastic over the bottom piece.

6. Choose a colored ribbon that matches the inside and glue it lengthwise around the mezuzah, slightly left, off center.

III. USING MY MEZUZAH

- Time permitting, students can present and describe their mezuzah to the rest of the class.

- Using the instructions for affixing the mezuzah attached to this lesson, demonstrate to the students how and where to hang a mezuzah.

- Review and recite with the students the *b'rachah* for affixing the mezuzah.

- As a way to help the students focus on the goals of the past two sessions, stress once more the connection between the mezuzah and memory/remembrance. Explain to them that a mezuzah is more than just a decorative, pretty object: it is a symbol meant to remind us of something good and important we don't ever want to forget. Noticing our mezuzot as we walk into a room is a way to remember God, the Israelites, freedom, and other special things in our lives.

Homework

Students should have to affix the mezuzah by a room of their choice. Once they have done so, students should do the following exercise:

1. During the week, as you enter this room, try to notice the mezuzah and think about what it reminds you of.

2. Pass by and pay attention to your mezuzah for a few days before answering the following questions:

   • When I notice my mezuzah, I think about …

   • What do I feel when I think about the special things my mezuzah reminds me of?

   • What other Jewish ways do I have to remind myself of special things every day?

Affixing a mezuzah*

Recite blessing for affixing a *mezuzah*:

Ba-ruch a-ta Adonai,

Eh-lo-hei-nu Meh-lech ha-o-lam,

a-sher ki-d'sha-nu b'mitz-vo-tzav

v'tzi-va-nu lik-bo-ah m'zu-zah

בָּרוּךְ אַתָּה יְיָ

אֱלֹהֵינוּ מֶלֶךְ הָעוֹלָם,

אֲשֶׁר קִדְּשָׁנוּ בְּמִצְוֹתָיו,

וְצִוָּנוּ לִקְבּוֹעַ מְזוּזָה.

We praise You, Eternal God, Sovereign of the universe: You hallow us with Your Mitzvot, and command us to affix the mezuzah.

The mezuzah, its top inclining inward, is affixed to the upper part of the doorpost (or on the nearby wall) on the right, as one enters the room. After affixing the mezuzah, it is customary to recite the *Shehecheyanu* blessing.

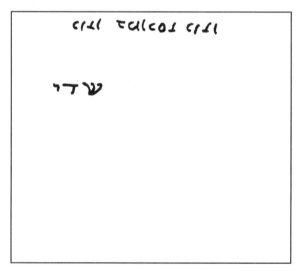

*Adapted from *On The Doorposts of Your House,* New York: CCAR Press, 1994.

Parashat B'shalach: Nachshon Comes to Visit

Introduction: Lesson Overview

The focus of this lesson, based on Exodus 14:10–18, 26–27, is on the miracle of the parting of the Sea of Reeds (Red Sea) that follows the Israelites escape from Egypt. The central question raised by the lesson is: *Where* is the real miracle in this biblical story? In God parting the sea, or in Nachshon's courage, according to the midrash, in stepping into the sea and risking his life? Students will have the opportunity to explore the Nachshon story and its implications, such as the power of taking a (reasonable) risk and the miracles we have the power to bring about in our lives.

Enduring Understanding

> ➤ Torah is an ongoing dialogue between the text and its students.

> ➤ Torah is real in our daily lives; it is with us wherever we are.

> ➤ Developing the skills to study Torah is essential to integrating Torah into our lives.

Essential Questions

1. What does the Torah have to say to me and to my world?

2. Why is the Torah different from other books?

3. How can Torah study help me in my everyday life?

Questions To Be Addressed

- What's the miracle in the text?

- What is God's role in the miracle? Moses' role? Nachshon's role?

- Are there miracles in our lives? What are they?

- Who makes the miracles in our lives happen?

- How does it make you feel that all of us can make miracles in our lives?

- How can you help others see the miracles they make happen in their lives?

Evidence of Understanding

- Students can make a connection between the Book of Exodus and Nachshon's story.

- Students are able to describe what they think Moses and Nachshon might have been feeling before and after the sea parted.

- Students are able to relate their own stories about miracles in their lives or in the lives of others they know.

- Students can draw a parallel between their experience and feelings and those of Moses and Nachshon.

- Students can articulate that the miracle at the sea might be more than just the work of God parting the waters, but that human beings also had a role in making the miracle happen and that we, too, can have a role in making miracles happen.

Staff/Material Needed

A guest (rabbi or parent) dressed up as Nachshon (see Activity III)

The Text

NOTE: The following is from *The Torah: A Modern Commentary*, W. G. Plaut ed. (New York: UAHC Press, 1981), and is meant for the teacher only.

10] As Pharaoh drew near, the Israelites caught sight of the Egyptians advancing upon them. Greatly frightened, the Israelites cried out to the LORD.

11] And they said to Moses, "Was it for want of graves in Egypt that you brought us to die in the wilderness? What have you done to us, taking us out of Egypt?

12 Is this not the very thing we told you in Egypt, saying, 'Let us be, and we will serve the Egyptians, for it is better for us to serve the Egyptians than to die in the wilderness'?"

13] But Moses said to the people, "Have no fear! Stand by, and witness the deliverance which the LORD will work for you today; for the Egyptians whom you see today you will never see again.

14] The LORD will battle for you; you hold your peace!"

15] Then the LORD said to Moses, "Why do you cry out to Me? Tell the Israelites to go forward.

16] And you lift up your rod and hold out your arm over the sea and split it, so that the Israelites may march into the sea on dry ground.

17] And I will stiffen the hearts of the Egyptians so that they go in after them; and I will assert My authority against Pharaoh and all his warriors, his chariots and his horsemen.

18] Let the Egyptians know that I am LORD, when I assert My authority against Pharaoh, his chariots, and his horsemen."

26] Then the LORD said to Moses, "Hold out your arm over the sea, that the waters may come back upon the Egyptians and upon their chariots and upon their horsemen."

27] Moses held out his arm over the sea, and at daybreak the sea returned to its normal state, and the Egyptians fled at its approach. But the LORD hurled the Egyptians into the sea.

Exodus 14:10-18, 26-27

ACTIVITY PLAN

I. SET INDUCTION

Goal

- To focus students on the special/important events of their lives and their role in making those happen

Activity

- Ask students to think about something unexpected that happened to them that turned out to be special or important.

Examples:

1. Leah went with her parents to visit their friends expecting to have a yucky time and discovered that there was a girl her age living next door. Leah didn't know the girl but decided to introduce herself and ended up having a great time. As a matter of fact, that girl is now Leah's best friend. What an amazing way to turn a yucky time into great fun and find a best friend too!

2. Ben's dad told him, "Always put your dog, Shemesh, on a leash when you go outside with her!" The other day, Ben was in a hurry and Shemesh really needed to go out, so he just took her outside without the leash. She ran into the street. A bicycle was coming but was able to stop in time, so nothing bad happened to Shemesh. Ben got really scared and felt very relieved when he realized that Shemesh was unhurt. From that moment on, Ben learned how to take much better care of and protect Shemesh. As he thought about it, Ben realized that a double miracle had happened that day: on the one hand, Shemesh was spared from an accident (that could have hurt her badly) and at the same time he himself had learned about being more responsible.

• Ask students to think about their own stories. If necessary they can write down a few words in order to remember them later.

Summary

Today we are going to think about special things that happen in our lives, and things that happened to the Israelites as they escaped from Egypt, where they were slaves.

The big question we're going to ask is:

> What makes an event special or important? What makes a miracle?

II.   THE STORY-TELLING

Goal

• To help students empathize with the plight of Moses and the Israelites.

Set Induction

• Ask the students to sit in a circle on the floor and get ready for a story. Tell the story of the escape from Egypt in a very suspenseful and dramatic manner. (See text on p. XX.) The story will end with the Israelites standing before the sea, the Egyptians behind them and the seawater in front of them.

• Ask the following question (record responses on board or on flipchart paper): You are an Israelite. How are you feeling right now?

III. SEEING MIRACLES: NACHSHON COMES TO VISIT*

• Ask a special guest (rabbi or parent) to dress up as Nachshon and come to class to tell "his" midrash, his interpretation of the Exodus story. "Nachshon" should enter as the students are talking about their feelings, and sit or stand while the discussion goes on. Then, he can introduce himself, or the teacher can ask, "Excuse me, sir, who are you and what are you doing here?" as a way to help Nachshon start his tale.

NOTE: "Nachshon" can also relate what Moses did by reading the following text—a simplified version of the text from Exodus 14:13, 15.

> 13] But Moses said to the people: "Have no fear! Watch and you will see how God saves you today; for the Egyptians you see here today you will never see again."

> 15] Then God said to Moses: "Why do you cry out to Me? Tell the Israelites to go forward."

• Nachshon will explain to the students that NOBODY wanted to go forward and he just *had* to do something about it… So, he walked in to his knees, his elbows, his shoulders, his chin… all the way past his nose. Just as he thought it was all over, the water started to move and actually split in two and he could breathe again.

• As part of his story, Nachshon should lead the children in singing *Mi Chamochah*. As part of the teaching, he might also tell the following midrash regarding the pronunciation of this prayer.

NOTE: The following midrash may be considered an enrichment text. It is up to the teacher to decide whether or not to use it, depending on the needs and level of each specific class. In case the teacher decides to use this text, he or she should explain to the students that a midrash is a sort of legend, or story, that helps us better understand the words and events described in the Torah.

Midrash

• Why do we say *"Mi chamochah"* when singing the first line of the *Mi Chamochah* prayer, and *"Mi kamochah"* in the second line? Here is the story why:

*See background on p. 71

As Nachshon was going into the sea and the waters had reached up to his neck, he started singing to God. By the time he got to the second line of his song, the water was already up to his nose and impeded him from getting out the right Hebrew sound *ch* for the word *"chamocha"*—and all that came out from Nachshon's throat instead was the *k* sound. This is why today we still say *"Mi chamochah"* for the first line of the prayer, and *"Mi kamochah"* in the second line.

Nachshon's Conclusions

- Upon telling his story, Nachshon can reflect on how amazed he was that he, a regular guy, was able to do something so important. He knows that people have said that the miracle happened because he walked into the sea. Nachshon can ask the students if they have any questions for him.

Questions For Discussion

("Nachshon" can ask this question or leave it to the teacher)

Where do students see the miracle: in Nachshon's walking into the sea or in God's making the waters part?

Conclusion

The teacher should introduce the following exercises and ask the students to complete the "In Class" activity as the summary of the lesson. The second piece is to be done at home with a parent.

In Class

In their TORAH JOURNAL, students should write or draw the "miracle" from their own miracle story. "Nachshon" and the teacher will circulate as students are working, helping them formulate and articulate their stories.

At Home

Students will bring their miracle page home, relate their stories to their parent(s) and, together, will complete the following statement:

This story of miracles made me think of...

The Story of the Exodus

The Israelites (that's what the Jews used to be called) were slaves in Egypt. It was bad, bad, bad! Pharaoh (the king of Egypt) was very unhappy with the Israelites. He had noticed that the Israelites had many children and became afraid that if their number kept growing, this people would become more and more numerous, stronger and stronger, and eventually, one day, might even take over the power in Egypt. He did everything he could to get rid of the Israelites. One of his terrible measures to prevent the growth of the people of Israel had been the order to kill all the Jewish baby boys.

Exactly at this time, an Israelite boy was born in Egypt. His mother was afraid that the Pharaoh's men would kill him, too. So she hid him in a basket and placed it by the bank of the Nile River among the reeds that grew there. Sure enough, Pharaoh's daughter went to the river one day accompanied by her maidens and saw the basket stuck in the reedy water. She took the baby, brought him to the palace and raised him as if he were her own son. The child was named Moses.

Moses grew up as an Egyptian at Pharaoh's court with his adoptive mother. One day, young Moses saw an Egyptian beating a Hebrew (as the Israelites are referred to in the bible). The scene upset him so much that Moses reacted by striking and killing the Egyptian. Not knowing what to do next, he ran away to Midian, a city in the desert east of the Jordan River.

In Egypt, the Israelites were suffering a lot. After forty years that Moses had been living in Midian, God talked to him and ordered Moses to go back to Egypt and tell Pharaoh to free the Israelites from their slavery. Although this was a great idea, it made Moses extremely nervous because he knew that Pharaoh wasn't an easy person to deal with.

Moses went to Pharaoh and tried to tell him that the best thing to do was to listen to God and to let the Israelites go free. Obviously, Pharaoh ignored him. So, God, with Moses' help, sent ten plagues to Egypt to convince Pharaoh to release the Israelites.

First there was the blood plague. God made all the waters in the land of Egypt turn into blood. Then came frogs, which jumped everywhere (even on Pharaoh's pillow), but still Pharaoh didn't let the Israelites go. Then came lice. Still Pharaoh didn't give up. Next came wild beasts, trampling everyone and everything. Pharaoh would not budge. As if all that weren't enough, the cattle and other animals were killed by the next plague, which was followed by a huge hailstorm after which multitudes of locusts invaded everything and ate all the plants and crops in the fields. You would think that Pharaoh would smarten up and let the Israelites go by then… no dice.

The ninth plague was darkness. All of a sudden the day turned into the darkest of nights. Any attempt to make light was useless. It was very, very scary. Still Pharaoh wouldn't let the Israelites go free.

In the end, God sent the tenth plague. The tenth plague consisted of the killing of all the first-born of Egypt, human or animal. This included Pharaoh's first-born son as well. At that point, at last, Pharaoh told the Israelites, "Go, leave, get out of my sight. Right now. Go!"

Led by Moses, the Israelites left Egypt as quickly as they could. They took only what they could carry. They grabbed loaves of bread that hadn't had time to leaven properly and were still flat—that is what we call matzah (the unleavened bread that reminds us of the haste with which the Hebrews left Egypt, and their slavery, behind). Some say that over 600,000 Israelites left Egypt that day. The Egyptians were so happy to see them go that they gave them gold and jewelry, perhaps hoping that they'd never, ever return to Egypt.

The Israelites marched right into the desert, very excited to be free at last. After a while they saw a sea in front of them—*Yam Suf,* the Sea of Reeds. They would just have to figure out a way to cross the sea. All of a sudden they heard a noise… and the noise was getting louder and louder. People turned around and they saw Egyptian soldiers on horseback riding toward them through the desert—they had been sent to persecute the fleeing Hebrews once more. The Israelites looked in front of them and saw the Sea of Reeds… looked back and saw Pharaoh's threatening armies approaching fast. What could they do? They were surely going to die if they proceeded in those perilous waters, and they would die if they were reached by the soldiers. Where was God? Where was Moses?

Question:

After saying these last words, Nachshon (or the teacher) asks the students:

> You are an Israelite. What are your feelings right now?

Background for Teacher and "Nachshon" Actor

"It is taught that Rebbe Meir said: 'When the Israelites stood at the Sea of Reeds, the twelve tribes were fighting with one another with one saying: "I will be the first to go into the sea" and another saying, "No, I'll be the first to go down into the sea." As they stood there fighting, the tribe of Benjamin stepped up and walked right into the sea.' "

"Well," said Rebbe Judah to Rebbe Meir, "that is not quite how it happened. In fact, one tribe said, 'I will not be the first to step into the water,' and another tribe said, 'I will not be the first to step into the water.' While they were standing there fighting [with the Egyptians getting closer and closer and closer], Nachshon, the son of Aminadav [from the tribe of Judah] stepped forward and was the first to go into the sea. He went in up to his knees, then his waist, then his shoulders. Then his neck was under water, then his chin and his mouth and, finally, his nose was under water and he couldn't breathe. At that very moment, when Nachshon couldn't breathe anymore, the sea parted and the Israelites could escape." Later, when the Egyptians tried to walk through the dry part of the sea, the waters closed upon them and they couldn't catch the Israelites.

Babylonian Talmud: B. *Sotah*, 36b-37a.

Parashat Yitro: Helping Hands

Introduction: Lesson Overview

This lesson, based on Exodus 18:13–22 and Deuteronomy 1:13, seeks to impart the understanding that even great people like Moses need help and that there are more and less effective ways of offering it. Students will examine the ways in which Yitro, Moses' father-in-law, was able to help Moses, and through this story and a collaborative activity students will reflect upon and draw conclusions about what makes a good helper. Finally, by remembering a situation in which they have needed help—and thinking about what kind of help could have been useful at the time—students will bring into their own lives what they have just learned in this lesson.

Enduring understanding

➤ Torah is an ongoing dialogue between the text and its students.

➤ Torah is real in our daily lives; it is with us wherever we are.

➤ Developing the skills to study Torah is essential to integrating Torah into our lives.

Essential Questions

1. What does the Torah have to say to me and to my world?

2. Why is the Torah different from other books?

3. How can Torah study help me in my everyday life?

Questions To Be Addressed

• If God picks Moses to be a leader because he is so great, why does Moses need help?

• Is Moses seen as weak, either by God or by his people, because he needs help?

- Who does Moses see as a good helper?

- When is a good time to ask for help from others?

- What are the characteristics of a good helper?

- How do you decide who is the best helper for you?

Evidence of Understanding

- Students are able to articulate that even Moses, perhaps the greatest leader of the Jewish people, couldn't do everything by himself and needed help.

- Students are able to advise Moses about how to get some help.

- Students are able, by comparing Exodus 18:21 and Deuteronomy 1:13, to come up with a list of characteristics that the Torah thinks make someone a good helper.

- Students are able, by performing a task in group, to discern what characteristics they think make someone a good helper.

- Students are able to describe a time when they needed help and didn't ask for it, and then to describe who might have been a good helper for them and why.

Materials Needed

- Legos, Tinker Toys, K'nex: any building materials with which students can carry out the collaborative task of creating something of the teacher's choosing

- "Moses Gets Some Help" text (pp. 79–80)—only to be acted out and not replicable for students

The Text

NOTE: The following is from *The Torah: A Modern Commentary*, W. G. Plaut ed. (New York: UAHC Press, 1981), and is meant for the teacher only. The teacher should feel free to modify and simplify the story in order to facilitate the class' understanding.

13] Next day, Moses sat as magistrate among the people, while the people stood about Moses from morning until evening. 14] But when Moses' father-in-law saw how much he had to do for the people, he said, "What is this thing that you are doing to the people? Why do you act alone, while all the people stand about you from morning until evening?" 15] Moses replied to his father-in-law, "It is because the people come to me to inquire of God. 16] When they have a dispute, it comes before me, and I decide between a man and his neighbor, and I make known the laws and teachings of God."

17] But Moses' father-in-law said to him, "The thing you are doing is not right; 18] you will surely wear yourself out, and these people as well. For the task is too heavy for you; you cannot do it alone. 19] Now listen to me. I will give you counsel, and God be with you! You represent the people before God: you bring the disputes before God, 20] and enjoin upon them the laws and the teachings, and make known to them the way they are to go and the practices they are to follow. 21] You shall also seek out from among all the people capable men who fear God, trustworthy men who spurn ill-gotten gain. Set these over them as chiefs of thousands, hundreds, fifties, and tens, and 22] let them judge the people at all times. Have them bring every major dispute to you, but let them decide every minor dispute themselves. Make it easier for yourself, and let them share the burden with you.

Exodus 18:13–22

The following is a supplementary text, which deepens our understanding of the Torah's perception of a good judge. The following excerpt is taken from Moses' words to the Israelites just before they are to enter the Promised Land.

13] Pick from each of your tribes men who are wise, discerning and experienced, and I will appoint them as your heads.

Deuteronomy 1:13

ACTIVITY PLAN

I. Set Induction

Goals

- To familiarize students with the biblical text
- To understand that asking for help is not a sign of weakness
- To help students identify who is a good helper and whom to turn to in case of need
- To help students start thinking of themselves as helpers—people others might need—and figure out how to be up to the task

Activity: Moses Has a Problem

Students will be able to articulate that Moses has too much to do and will advise him on how to lessen his workload.

1. Begin with a dramatic statement such as:

   "Oy, Moses has a problem and needs our help. Here's what's happening…"

2. Read a modified version based on the biblical text (see pp. 73–74), stopping at verse 18.

3. Ask students these questions: What is Moses' problem? Why does Moses need help? (Answers may include: no one can do everything alone; we all need someone else's help at some point or other; when we are caught up in a big problem, it can be hard to see the solution—no matter how great and smart we are—and someone else's help can open our eyes and make it easier for us to see the solution.)

4. After a short discussion, ask students to come up with a solution to help Moses get all his work done. The teacher should write the students' suggestions on the board.

5. Students can then discuss the pros and cons of the ideas posted on the board, and try to agree on which solutions would be most effective.

6. Once students agree on an idea, read aloud the modified version of the biblical text in its entirety (or have students read it aloud, depending on the class' reading level).

Questions for Discussion

Who helped Moses solve his problem?

- What did Moses' father-in-law, Yitro, suggest?

- In what way is this similar to or different from our class' suggestion?

- Which solution do you prefer? Why?

II. FINDING A GOOD HELPER

Goals

- By engaging in a planning and building exercise, students will attempt to discern what makes a good helper.

- Students will compose their own list of characteristics of a good helper.

- Students will compare their list with the list in Exodus and the list in Deuteronomy.

Activity

1. Divide students into groups of four or five (preferably five). In particularly small classes, try to make groups no smaller than three students.

2. Using Legos or Tinker Toys or some other type of building toy, ask students to come up with a specific item, but don't give them a particular design or instructions. Working on the floor might be easier, especially if there is a carpeted area. For example, ask students to build a house, a car, a tree, or anything else of their choosing. Groups do not have to build the same item if there is a sense that different groups will enjoy different building projects. The suggested item should be complex enough to force students to plan it before building it. Their projects might later go on display in the classroom or elsewhere, labeled "GRADE 2 WORKS TOGETHER: LIKE MOSES AND THE JUDGES."

Instructions for Groups

• Build the item.

• As you are building, think about how you can best help the project move forward.

• You have 15 minutes to build this item.

Instructions for Teacher

While students are building, walk around the room, paying close attention to how they are working together as a group and what characteristics students are exhibiting as they help each other (or don't help each other, as the case may be).

3. Once groups have finished building (about 10-15 minutes), gather everybody together in a circle (preferably on the floor).

4. Ask each group to briefly show the class what it built.

Questions for Discussion

1. While you were working, you were asked to think about how you could best help the project move forward. Thinking back on how your group worked, what made you, or others in the group, a good helper (or a good partner)?

    NOTE: The teacher should make a list of characteristics on a big piece of paper in front of the students on the floor.

2. What made it easier to get your job done? (people's behaviors, characteristics, attitudes)

3. What made it harder to get your job done?

> NOTE: Ask students *not* to use other students' names when answering this question.

Students return to their seats. Projects are placed on a table as they return.

III. My Idea of a Good Helper

Goals

- To help students create their own list of characteristics of a good helper.

- To enable students to apply this list to a real situation in their lives.

Activity

1. Hand out sheets with the list of characteristics that Yitro described to Moses in Exodus 18:21 and the list Moses gave the Israelites in Deuteronomy 1:13 (see p. 81).

   > NOTE: The teacher might want to make a poster-size version of the list and add to it during the discussion described below.

2. Read through the list with the students, checking for understanding. Ask them: Why do you think that these characteristics make someone a good helper? What characteristics would you add? (Teacher can note them on the poster.)

   > NOTE: Students might raise questions about the characteristics of God: "How is God a good helper?" for example. Teachers should encourage students to answer such questions.

3. Hang up the list just compiled by the students.

Conclusion

- Ask students to complete the in-class portion of the TORAH JOURNAL and, if there is time, have them share and compare some of their answers with those from the *parashah* studied. Otherwise, students can complete both sections of the TORAH JOURNAL at home.

- As a summary comment the teacher can note: No matter how big or small, rich or poor we are, we all need help and we can all help others.

Homework

In Class

In their TORAH JOURNAL, ask students to make their own list of characteristics of good helpers, referring to the Torah's list and the list they made. They will also have to answer the question, "What characteristics will help me be a good partner to people who need help?" Students can share their lists with the class if they wish.

At Home

- Students should sit down with their parent(s) and talk about a time when they needed help and didn't ask for it. They should then write about it in their TORAH JOURNAL on the page that begins: "I was like Moses because I needed help. Here's what I needed help with…"

- Using the list of characteristics of a good helper, students should describe a person who helped them when they needed help. They should articulate what aspects of this person's character were particularly helpful in that situation (i.e. patience, kindness, being practical).

Moses has too much to do by himself. The following is a story from the Book of Exodus illustrating how Moses solved this problem.

Moses gets some help

Based on Exodus 18

The next day, Moses sat, helping people solve their problems (he was a judge). The line of people needing help was so long that Moses worked from morning until evening (without even a lunch break!).

When Moses' father-in-law saw how much work Moses had to do he said, "What on earth are you doing for all these people, Moses? And why are you doing it all by yourself, while everyone hangs around you from morning until evening?"

Moses replied to his father-in-law, "I must do this because people keep coming to me to solve their disagreements and I, as a judge who also knows what God wants and actually even speaks to God (as everybody already knows around here), must sit here all day long to listen and give answers. When they have a disagreement, they bring it to me and I decide what they should do, and I explain to them God's laws and teachings."
But Moses' father-in-law said to him, "What you are

doing just isn't right. You will definitely wear yourself out and wear the people out as well. It's totally exhausting for them to stand around all day waiting for you. This job is just too much for you; you can't do it alone."

What should have Moses done? [*Allow pause for students' responses*]

Moses' father-in-law continued: "Now, listen to me. I will give you advice and God be with you. You represent the people before God; you bring disagreements to God and point out to the people the laws and teachings they need to know and tell them what they should do and how they should do it.

"You should also pick out people to help you. Pick them from among the Israelites. These helpers should be capable and know how to do things, they must be people who recognize that God is truly awesome, people you can trust and who are not greedy. Put them in charge of thousands of people, hundreds of people, and so on. They will help people at all times. You can take care of the most serious and complicated cases, while these helpers can take care of all other easier cases at all times. Make it easier for yourself, and share the burden of this hard job with these capable helpers."

Characteristics of a Good Helper

According to Yitro (Exodus 18:21)	According to Moses (Deuteronomy 1:13)
• capable (knows what to do and can get things done)	• wise
• recognizes that God is truly awesome (inspiring, very impressive)	• knows what's right and wrong
• trustworthy	• has experience in life
• not greedy	

Parashat Ki Tisa: Hold On To Your Hat, God!

Introduction: Lesson Overview

This lesson, based on Exodus 32:1–14, provides a new and interesting angle for looking at the relationship between Moses and God. In *Parashat Ki Tisa*, Moses plays a central role in calming God, who is extremely angry at the Israelites. Students may be surprised that God needs to be calmed down by Moses. Their questions about this story can spawn an interesting discussion about what happens when we get angry with God—not only does God not punish us, but God actually listens to our reasons!

The goal for the students is to utilize the scenario between God and Moses to better understand how one calms down or can help calm someone else down when she or he is angry. The lesson draws on two texts—the primary one from the Book of *Sh'mot* (Exodus) and the secondary one from *D'varim* (Deuteronomy)—which demonstrate the effective and ineffective techniques Moses uses to defuse God's anger. The students are then asked to apply these techniques to their own lives.

Enduring Understanding

➤ Torah is an ongoing dialogue between the text and its students.

➤ Torah is real in our daily lives; it is with us wherever we are.

➤ Developing the skills to study Torah is essential to integrating Torah into our lives.

Essential Questions

1. What does the Torah have to say to me and to my world?

2. Why is the Torah different from other books?

3. How can Torah study help me in my everyday life?

Questions To Be Addressed

- Why does God get so angry at the Israelites?

- What does Moses do that is so effective in calming God?

- Why is Moses willing to try to calm God?

- What makes you angry?

- What did you learn from Moses' success in calming God that you can use to calm yourself down more easily, or to help calm other people when they are angry?

Evidence of Understanding

- Students will be able to help Moses think through ways to "calm God down."

- Students will be able to discern the effective and ineffective techniques used by Moses for calming God down when God is angry with the Israelites, and then apply the effective techniques to real-life situations.

- Students will be able to articulate multiple techniques for helping themselves or others to calm down and feel better after they have been upset. The techniques will be gleaned from the text, from interactive theater, and from discussions among the students.

Staff/Materials Needed

- Costumes for Moses and God

- Two actors (for Moses and God's roles)

The Text

NOTE: The following is from *The Torah: A Modern Commentary*, W. G. Plaut ed. (New York: UAHC Press, 1981), and is meant for the teacher only. The students' version of the text is in the form of interactive theater (see pp. 89–91).

> 1] When the people saw that Moses was so long in coming down from the mountain, the people gathered against Aaron and said to him, "Come, make us a god who shall go before us, for that man Moses, who brought us from the land of Egypt—we do not know what has happened to him." 2] Aaron said to them, "Take off the gold rings that are on the ears of your wives, your sons, and your daughters, and bring them to me." …

4] This he took from them and cast in a mold and made it into a molten calf. And they exclaimed, "This is your god, O Israel, who brought you out of the land of Egypt!" …

7] The LORD spoke to Moses, "Hurry down, for your people, whom you brought out of the land of Egypt, have acted basely. 8] They have been quick to turn aside from the way that I enjoined upon them. They have made themselves a molten calf and bowed low to it and sacrificed to it, saying: 'This is your god, O Israel, who brought you out of the land of Egypt!'"

9] The LORD further said to Moses, "I see that this is a stiffnecked people. 10] Now, let Me be, that My anger may blaze forth against them and that I may destroy them, and make of you a great nation." 11] But Moses implored the LORD his God, saying, "Let not Your anger, O LORD, blaze forth against Your people, whom You delivered from the land of Egypt with great power and with a mighty hand. 12] Let not the Egyptians say, 'It was with evil intent that He delivered them, only to kill them off in the mountains and annihilate them from the face of the earth.' Turn from Your blazing anger, and renounce the plan to punish Your people. 13] Remember Your servants, Abraham, Isaac, and Jacob, how You swore to them by Your Self and said to them: I will make your offspring as numerous as the stars of heaven, and I will give to your offspring this whole land of which I spoke, to possess forever." 14] And the LORD renounced the punishment He had planned to bring upon His people.

Exodus Chapter 32:1–2, 4, 7–14

ACTIVITY PLAN

I.   SET INDUCTION

- Ask students to write a scenario about an incident when they got mad and someone tried to calm them down in a way that didn't work. (See worksheet on page 88 designed to help them write it out.) Tell the students that anyone who wishes to share his or her story with the rest of the class will be able to do so later.

    NOTE: If it is too difficult for students to write this, teachers can ask a few students to describe a scenario and summarize it for them in one or two sentences on the board or flipchart paper.

- Collect the worksheets for later use.

II. INTERACTIVE THEATER

Goals

- To familiarize students with the biblical text—specifically Moses' skill in calming God

- To help students discern between more and less effective ways of dealing with anger

Activity

Interactive theater is a mechanism through which students can become part of the action in a given scenario. The performers interact with the students and allow the students to switch places with them.

Performers

Ideally, older students (high-school age) should come to class and take on the roles in the scenario. Otherwise, three or four parents can take on the roles.

Action

- Using the attached scenario, act out the initial scenes.

- Stop action and, in roles, have actors ask the students the questions embedded in the scenario.

- Teachers should facilitate the discussion when necessary. The teacher should also write down students' answers to the questions on the board/flipchart paper.

- At the end of the play, the actors might want to take additional questions in character from the students.

    NOTE: Actors should try to engage the students as much as possible. If students seem to have an idea for doing a better job, let them come up and play the part of Moses.

Wrap-Up Discussion of Theater Activity

Looking at the lists of "calming techniques" from both the ineffective and effective scenarios, ask the students the following:

- How do you think Moses was feeling as he tried to convince God not to destroy the Israelites?

- Why is it scary or uncomfortable to approach someone when she or he is really angry?

- What do you think helped Moses be brave when he approached God?

- What did you learn from Moses about helping to calm angry people?

- How might what you learned today help you calm someone else down?

III. BECOMING MOSES: HELPING OTHERS WHO ARE ANGRY

Goal

- Drawing on the previous activity and using the real-life scenarios that students wrote at beginning of class, students will come up with ways to help others who are angry.

Activity

1. Divide students into groups of three.

2. Each group should receive one scenario written by a student at the beginning of the class; choose one of the scenarios noted on the flipchart paper/board; or come up with a new one.

3. Ask students to attempt to address the situation described in the scenario and come up with a plan of action (10 minutes). (See specific instructions on p. 88.)

4. Choose 2 or 3 groups to describe to the rest of the class their idea for calming the person down. The student who wrote the scenario (or the class as a whole) can respond to the group's suggestions regarding their effectiveness and other potential ideas.

Conclusion

- Summarize the students' comments.

- Point out the risk that Moses took in talking to God when God was so angry. (Compare it to the fear one might have about addressing an angry parent or friend.)

- Assign TORAH JOURNAL exercise to do in class or as homework.

Homework

In Class or At Home

In your Torah Journal, write one or two pieces of advice you could use the next time you have to deal with someone who is angry (with you, or with someone else):

1._____

_____

_____

_____

_____

2._____

_____

_____

_____

Grrrrrr, That Made Me So Mad!

Think of a time when you were really mad about something or at someone, and a friend or relative tried to calm you down to make you feel better but, instead, made you even *angrier*!

NOTE: Your example, with your permission, might be shared with the rest of the class.

Write down in two sentences what made you mad about that particular situation.

_____

_____

_____

_____

_____

_____

Hold On To Your Hat, God!

Characters

Moses and God

Action

Moses is sitting down while God slowly paces back and forth, clearly immersed in deep thoughts. God is dictating something (the Ten Commandments) to Moses, who is writing everything down carefully.

MOSES: God, could you please repeat that last line, you know, the one about not wanting other people's stuff… I didn't quite catch the word.

GOD: I said, "You shall not *covet*." C-O-V-E-T, got it?

MOSES: Okay. Got it. That's ten, total. Are there any more?

God: No. I think that pretty much covers it. It'll take a while for the people of Israel to get used to these rules. I wouldn't want to complicate things by adding more. Ten is a nice round number… Hey, what's going on down there? Moses, quick, take a look!

Moses looks at where God is pointing and gets a look of horror on his face.

GOD (*in great anger*): I can't believe it! They are dancing around a golden calf and calling it god…What is going on here? *I* am the only God!

MOSES (*muttering*): I can't believe that brother of mine… what was Aaron thinking… I'm going to….

GOD (*interrupting*): Hurry down, for YOUR people… you know, the ones YOU brought out of the land of Egypt… have done something VERY bad. It didn't take them very long to disobey Me. Look what they have done: they have made themselves a calf out of gold and they are bowing down to it. The Israelites are a very stubborn people—they just don't learn. Look Moses, just go away so that I can destroy them and show them how angry I am…

Moses turns to the students and speaks directly to them. In the meantime, God is in the background pacing and fuming.

MOSES (*looking at the students*): Oy! I can't believe this. I returned to Egypt from Midian (where I was having a quiet, peaceful life), I went to Pharaoh, got involved with all those messy, yucky plagues, rushed 600,000 people out of Egypt at a moment's notice, walked through a horrendous sea that I think is going to drown us all at any minute... and what do I get for it? What do they do? They get God all mad by worshipping a golden calf...a CALF of all things, I hate cows! Oy! Now I have to try to stop God from destroying them... because as annoying as these fools are, they are still the Israelites, my people, God's people. But how do I do this? What can *I* do to stop God? Plus, I'm not just talking to any "Joe Shmoe" on the street. This is *God*. What if God gets mad at ME and I get destroyed? I'm just a little bit nervous here. You look like intelligent people... Maybe you can help me. What can I do or say to keep God from killing all these people? Are there any volunteers to talk to God? Maybe you can do a better job than I.

Moses encourages the students to convince God not to destroy the people of Israel.

> NOTE TO THE TEACHER AND ACTORS: Each student who volunteers should approach God and make her or his argument. God should respond gently, with humor, but not be convinced by the student's suggestions. Students should be given about a minute each to convince God. If some students are too shy to go up in front of the group, they can whisper their idea to Moses and Moses can try it out on God.
>
> As students are pleading the cause of the Israelites to God, the teacher should write down the main points of each argument on the board or on flipchart paper. After several, or all, students have "conversed" with God, Moses thanks the students and resumes his dialogue with God.

MOSES: Those were fabulous ideas. Don't you agree with me, God?

GOD: They really were great ideas and, maybe, just maybe, I'll change my mind. But, I'm still really mad. Give me one more good reason, Moses, just WHY I should spare this stubborn people.

MOSES (*if the reasons he is about to give God were also among the students' suggestions, Moses should point this out as he speaks*): I beg you God, DON'T DO IT! You went through all the trouble of saving them from Egypt with your great power and Your strong and mighty hand. Do You want the Egyptians to say that You brought them out of Egypt just to kill them in the mountains and wipe them off the face of the earth? That wouldn't make You look really good, would it? I can hear the Egyptians now: "Can you believe that the Israelites' God went through all the trouble to get this people out of our hands, to bring them out of here, only to kill them in the desert? Our powerful Pharaoh could have done just the same, only more efficiently... they wouldn't have had to run anywhere, we could have killed them here on the spot... one, two, three... done with it! What an illogical God!" Don't You think that this is what everybody is going to say? Besides, God, I know you hate breaking promises. As a matter of fact, You have NEVER, EVER broken a promise. Remember, You promised to Abraham, Isaac, and Jacob that You would make sure they had as many descendants as there are stars in the sky? And do You remember Your promise to give them a whole land? Well, God, it doesn't seem to me that destroying this people is something You really want to do. It would ruin Your reputation as a just, loving God who keeps promises.

GOD: Well, Moses, you and these kids made a pretty good argument. I am still a bit mad. I don't think they should be let totally off the hook. I want them to understand that there are rules and you can't go unpunished when you break promises or rules. But, I won't destroy them. Thanks for your help on this one, Moses. Something really sad could have happened if you were not so smart to help me calm down a little and reconsider things before acting upon a moment's anger. I hate it when my anger gets the best of me.

Parashat Mishpatim: Reaching Out To Strangers

Introduction: Lesson Overview

This lesson is based upon two verses from the Torah portion *Mishpatim* (*lit.* laws) that regard welcoming strangers (Exodus 22:20 and 23:9). The term "stranger," for the sake of this lesson, is defined in two ways: 1) a newcomer, someone unknown to the community or the individual, and 2) someone who looks or acts differently from most other people (wheelchair-bound person, visually impaired, mentally disabled, etc.).

The lesson is divided into two sections: text study and role-play activity. The goal of the text study is to frame the importance of welcoming strangers as expressed in the Torah. The goal of the role-play activity is to help students make a link between the law of welcoming the stranger and their lives today. As a summary to the lesson, students are asked to express two or three ways in which they and their community can help "strangers" feel welcome and/or accepted. The teacher may decide to share the list of students' ideas with the rest of the community by posting them in a public space of the synagogue or at school.

This lesson is the last one of the Torah strand for second grade. At the end of this class, the teacher can choose to do one of the following: a) ceremonially complete the study of the Book of Exodus by reciting the traditional phrase used when completing a book of the Torah (see lesson plan); and/or b) devote some time to explaining to students their home assignment in which they are asked to reflect upon what they have learned about Torah (and from Torah) throughout this course.

Enduring Understanding

➤ Torah is an ongoing dialogue between the text and its students.

➤ Torah is real in our daily lives; it is with us wherever we are.

➤ Developing the skills to study Torah is essential to integrating Torah into our lives.

Essential Questions

1. What does the Torah have to say to me and to my world?

2. Why is the Torah different from other books?

3. How can Torah study help me in my everyday life?

Questions To Be Addressed

- Who is a stranger? What makes someone a "stranger"?

- Why do strangers/newcomers need to be welcomed?

- What kinds of things can we do to help strangers/newcomers feel welcome?

- In a situation in which you yourself were a stranger, what made you feel welcome?

- Which of the Torah portions you studied during the last several weeks was most important for your daily life? Why?

Evidence of Understanding

- Students will be able to put together a list of characteristics that define a "stranger"—a term that students will understand as indicating not only someone from a different country, but any newcomer or person who looks and acts differently from most other people.

- Students will be able to discuss and reflect upon the connection between how we treat "strangers" today and the experience of the Israelites in Egypt as related in *Sh'mot* (Book of Exodus) 22:20 and 23:9.

- Through a role-playing activity, students will be able to demonstrate their empathy with "strangers" and determine ways to welcome them.

- Based on their own past experiences as "strangers" and/or "newcomers," students will be able to formulate a few suggestions about how to help strangers feel welcome and accepted.

- Students will be able to articulate the most important personal learning they took away from the nine Torah lessons studied as part of this second-grade curriculum, and to give reasons why this learning continues to be important in their lives.

Staff/Materials Needed

- High school students or parents to help with role plays

The Text

NOTE: The following is from *The Torah: A Modern Commentary*, W. G. Plaut ed. (New York: UAHC Press, 1981), and is meant for the teacher only. The biblical text provided for the students on p. 102—based on this same version—has been modified and simplified in order to facilitate the class' understanding of story.

> *You shall not wrong* [mistreat] *a stranger or oppress* [put down, humiliate] *him, for you were strangers in the land of Egypt.*

Exodus 22:20

> *You shall not oppress* [put down, humiliate] *a stranger, for you know the feelings of the stranger, having yourselves been strangers in the land of Egypt.*

Exodus 23:9

ACTIVITY PLAN

I. SET INDUCTION

Goal

- Students will be introduced to the concept of "stranger" as indicating someone who is new to the community, who is unknown to them.

Introduction

- Explain to students:

  This Torah portion includes many rules to help us conduct our lives properly and to make our world a happier place. One important rule involves making everybody feel welcome and accepted within our community (at school, in our town, in our family, etc.). There are two verses that teach us about making strangers feel welcome among us.

- Have students answer the following questions: Who is a stranger? What characteristics define a "stranger"?

NOTE: Most students will assume that a stranger is any adult they don't know and should stay away from or avoid talking to. The teacher should help students understand that children they don't know can also be defined as "strangers," as well as adults who are known to their parents but not to them. The teacher may also want to send a note home to the children's parents explaining the way in which the term "stranger" is being used in this lesson, as a way to differentiate the stranger we want children to stay away from and the stranger we want to welcome.

- Allow time for the students to develop the concept of who is a stranger. The teacher should write on the board a list of attributes that will help students understand who can be defined a stranger:

  A person you don't know yet (someone who has been in your school, synagogue or neighborhood, but you weren't friends with)

  A person who lived somewhere else before joining your community (someone who just moved to your school, synagogue, or neighborhood)

  A person who speaks a different language (someone who just moved to your school, synagogue, or neighborhood from a different country)

  A person who looks or acts differently (because of his or her race, or because of specific physical traits or handicaps—such as someone in a wheelchair, blind, deaf, who uses sign language, or who is affected by mental disability)

II. TEXT STUDY

Goals

- To articulate the importance of making newcomers, and all those who are different, feel welcome and accepted

- To make a connection between the unwelcoming life-conditions for the Israelites in Egypt (where they were strangers and suffered a lot) and the situation of present-day "strangers" within our communities (toward whom, as Jews, we are committed to behave in a welcoming, accepting manner)

Activity

1. Hand out copies of Exodus 22:20 and 23:9 and read the verses aloud to the students:

   "You shall not make a stranger feel bad or treat him or her poorly, because you were strangers in the land of Egypt." (Exodus 22:20)

"You shall not treat a stranger poorly, for you know the feelings of the stranger, having your-selves been strangers in the land of Egypt." (Exodus 23:9)

2. Analyze and discuss the texts with the students. Ask the following:

- Thinking about Moses' struggles to get the Jewish people out of the land of Egypt, it is clear that the Jews must have been very unhappy there: Why do you think they were unhappy?

- Why do these verses say, "*You* were strangers in the land of Egypt"? *We*, the people in this class today, have personally never lived in Egypt. Why should "we" be made part of this?

- What does having been strangers in Egypt have to do with how we treat strangers today?

Summary of Discussion

- Remind the students of the story from the Passover Haggadah, in which we are asked to remember the times when we were not free, when we were strangers in a foreign land (a land that treated us badly) where we were slaves. Although today we are free to live, do and say what we like, the story of the Exodus from Egypt reminds us how hard it was to live in a place where we were not wanted, that wasn't our real home and where our freedom was taken away from us. The verses we studied today may help us remember to treat newcom-ers in a kind way—in the same way we wish the Egyptians had treated the Israelites when they were strangers in that land many centuries ago.

- Point out the following as questions the students can be thinking about during the next part of the lesson:

  What can we do to make strangers or newcomers feel welcome and accepted in our coun-try, community, home, school, and synagogue?

  What is the lesson we must learn from our Jewish past?

III. ACTIVITY: WELCOMING STRANGERS

Goal

- To enable students to think about how they can make a stranger feel welcome. Ask students the following:

- Think about someone who just moved to your neighborhood or town from somewhere else, or think about a time when you and your family moved to a new place. (If students have never moved from where they live, they could think of a vacation they took with their family abroad or to some place away from home.)

- Have you ever heard someone speaking a language other than English? How does it feel to be with someone, or even surrounded by people, who speak a language you don't understand?

- Think of a time when you went to a place where you didn't know anybody. Try to remember and describe the feelings you had as you arrived. Did you end up having a good time? If so, what made you feel better?

Role Play

Instructions

There are four role-play scenarios in this section (see pages 103–106). It would probably be enough to complete two or three role plays in order to maintain the focus and attention of the students. Some adults or older students will be needed to help out with this activity.

Divide students into groups of up to five people, with one adult or older student assigned to each group.

Distribute one scenario to each group.

> NOTE: Be aware of time limits. It is important that all groups get a chance to play out their scenarios. Make sure to carefully time this part of the lesson so as not to disappoint the students.

In each small group, the grown-up helper should:

1. read through the scenario with the students

2. make sure the students understand the issue

3. elicit ideas for potential solutions based on the questions at the end of the scenario

4. decide on one or two solutions to act out

5. design and practice the role playing (not all students have to act out the role play, if some feel uncomfortable doing so)

When groups have finished preparing, ask them to present their scenarios. After each group has had its turn, ask students to answer the following question:

> What is a good way to welcome a "stranger" according to what we have learned from watching these scenarios?

IV. WRAP-UP ACTIVITY: *PARASHAT MISHPATIM*

Goal

- To help students integrate the previous activities, and draw direct parallels to their own experiences as "strangers" (when they are in an environment different from their usual one)

Activity

1. Review all the things the students have said about what can be done to make a stranger feel welcome and part of their group.

2. Ask them the following question:

   Think of a time when someone did a good job in helping you feel welcome and not alone or left out. What made you feel welcome?

3. Ask students to share their answers to this question. The teacher should write the answers on pieces of construction paper or previously made puzzle pieces (see below). The teacher can write the students' ideas on sentence strips or pieces of construction paper as the groups share their lists. Duplicate ideas should be acknowledged but not written down.

4. The sentence strips will be placed around the room, or in other public spaces in the school, to remind everyone of the duty we have to make strangers feel welcome in our community, and of the various ways to obtain this goal.

5. Suggest to students to point their work out to their parents, siblings, and other friends as they walk around the synagogue. Tell them that, hopefully, their suggestions will help people (even grown-ups) learn something about turning the community into a friendlier, more welcoming place.

   NOTE: In those synagogues without a regular building, teachers might want to create a puzzle made out of many pieces. Each student's suggestion can be written on the puzzle pieces and posted on a board where slowly the entire puzzle will come together and be completed. For example, the teacher may want to create an earth-, tree-, or clasped-hands-shaped puzzle. The enduring understanding of this puzzle activity should be that by working together, we contribute to making our community a place that welcomes everybody—strangers or not.

VI. CONCLUSION: SUMMARY OF TORAH UNIT

- At the front of the room, line up the *parashah* cards from the Introduction to Torah lesson at the beginning of the Torah unit.

- Point out the six *parshiyot* (Torah portions) that the class studied (*Sh'mot, Bo, B'shalach, Yitro, Ki Tisa, Mishpatim*).

- Explain the following:

  This is the final lesson in our Torah unit about the book of *Sh'mot* (Exodus). Traditionally, when a scholar completes the study and the reading of one of the books of the Torah, the following Hebrew words are said:

  $$\text{חֲזַק חֲזַק וְנִתְחַזֵּק}$$

  Chazak, chazak v'nitchazeik!

  Be strong, be strong and may you be strengthened!

- Ask students to yell out the phrase several times as loud as they wish, with real strength!

- Ask them the following:

  Why do you think we speak about strength when we finish reading a book of the Torah?

    (Possible answers may include: because studying and reading Torah makes us stronger, and when we study it together we become even stronger.)

- Point out homework assignment to be done in the TORAH JOURNAL.

- End with a final repetition of: *Chazak, chazak v'nitchazeik* and wish the students MAZAL TOV! (congratulations) for completing their study of the book of *Sh'mot* (Exodus).

DATE_____

Dear Parents:

In class we discussed two verses from the Torah portion Mishpatim, which is found in Sh'mot (the Book of Exodus, 22:20 and 23:9). These verses teach us about our duty to welcome strangers into our midst, to make strangers (newcomers) feel accepted and at home. We learned about the times when the Jewish people were strangers in Egypt and mistreated in that land. But now that we are free and live in a place where we are fully accepted, we shouldn't forget to treat kindly and fairly those who are strangers in our land (community, family, school, or workplace). The class discussed that it is possible to make friends with people we didn't know before, and that welcoming these newcomers is a way of helping them feel accepted and of creating a happier, healthier community.

Sincerely

_____

Parashat Mishpatim:
Reaching Out To Strangers

Together with your parent(s), look back at the pages you filled out during this Torah course in your **TORAH JOURNAL** and answer the following two questions:

What was your favorite *parashah* (Torah portion)? Why?

_____

_____

_____

Of all the things you learned in and from the Torah, what do you think is the most important for your life? Why?

_____

_____

_____

חֲזַק חֲזַק וְנִתְחַזֵּק

CHAZAK, CHAZAK V'NITCHAZEK!

BE STRONG, BE STRONG
AND MAY YOU BE STRENGTHENED!

Parashat Mishpatim

"You shall not make a stranger feel bad or treat him or her poorly, because you were strangers in the land of Egypt."

(Exodus 22:20)

"You shall not treat a stranger poorly, for you know the feelings of the stranger, having yourselves been strangers in the land of Egypt."

(Exodus 23:9)

Role play 1

In our synagogue there are five second-graders who have been best friends since preschool. Today the teacher introduced the class to a new student, Rachel, who just moved here from Oklahoma. Rachel says hello and sits down at her desk. She doesn't talk to anyone around her. The bell rings for lunch. You and your four friends run to get in line. You go over to Rachel to ask her to join you, and immediately your friends start pointing at you and making funny faces. Rachel also sees your friends and notices that they are pointing at you in an unfriendly way.

- How do you feel? How do you think Rachel feels?
- What might you say to your friends?
- How can you help Rachel feel better?
- What do you think Rachel should do?

Role play 2

Ari has just moved to your town from Israel. You think he looks like a nice person. You go over to say hello and you realize Ari can't understand you. He smiles in a friendly way and says, "Ari no speak English." You take his strange way of expressing himself as a sign that Ari is not smart and you just walk away from him. Ari's smile turns into a really sad expression.

- How else could you have reacted to Ari?
- The fact that someone speaks a different language might make it harder for you to get to know each other. Can you think of other ways to get to know someone like Ari better?
- How could you approach Ari and help him feel better in this new place?

Role play 3

At your school, at lunchtime you and your friends always play kickball. Elliot, a younger boy from another class, asks you if he can play with you and your friends. He has never been part of your group. Elliot has never spoken to any of you before. You are afraid your friends will think you are weird because you want to play with younger kids. The guys are calling you: "Come on, hurry, let's play ball!" You know that soon your friends are going to get annoyed. But Elliot is looking at you, waiting for an answer, for some reaction to his question whether he can join your game or not.

- What do you say to him?
- What do you say to your friends?

Role play 4

You are in Sunday school with all your friends. Beth, a girl you have seen in your public school, comes into your class today with her mother. You have noticed that this girl attends the special education class in your school. You are curious about Beth because she sits in a wheelchair. It also looks very cool: she presses a button and her chair moves. But you have never said hello to her in school, though you have seen her many times. She takes a special bus that can accommodate her and her wheelchair. No one talks to these kids in school because they are different. Now she is in your class in synagogue. When your teacher moves a chair away and tells Beth to sit right next to you, your first thought is, "Oh, no!"

- What are your feelings about this situation?
- You have ignored Beth every time you saw her before. What are you going to do this time?
- Although she looks really strange in that chair, she turns to you and smiles. What is Beth thinking? How do you think she is feeling?
- How can you make Beth feel more comfortable?

Avodah

Deborah Niederman

Foreword

The essential teaching, or enduring understanding, at the heart of all the lessons in the *Avodah* strand of the *CHAI: Learning for Jewish Life* Curriculum Core can be synthesized as follows: *Avodah* is prayer, ceremonies, and celebrations. *Avodah* is the work we do to find sacred connections to God, community, and self. The Hebrew word *avodah* means "work," or "service." The Rabbis came to understand *avodah* not merely as physical labor, but as the spiritual work the mind and heart engage in to connect with God.

The focus for the second-grade lessons is on answering questions about God and developing skills to feel connected to God. Judaism offers us plenty of prayers, used for centuries, to connect with God, but some of these prayers are too difficult for young students to understand at this early age. It is therefore better to first explain and explore with them the "whats" and "hows" of the Hebrew God—to acquaint them with the God these prayers talk about and talk to. Students want to know what God looks like and sounds like; how they know for sure that God is talking to them; and, most important, how they can be sure that God hears what they are saying. The teacher's task is to provide opportunities for students to explore these questions. Teachers are encouraged to share their own answers, and when they don't have an answer, it is okay to say so. Through this open dialogue about and with God, students will learn that understanding God is a lifelong process.

Jewish tradition teaches us that one of the best ways to learn is through storytelling; to that end, several of the lessons for this curriculum's component are based on the stories from the book *Hello, Hello, Are You There, God?* by Molly Cone (New York: UAHC Press, 1999).[1] For our *avodah* lessons, the stories have been organized in a different order from the original book and have been interspersed with specific exercises and activities concerning chosen blessings. The lesson plans, focusing on deeply exploring the students' enduring understanding, have been modeled on the curriculum design methods developed in *Understanding by Design*[2].

Although there is a designated "evidence of understanding" for each individual lesson, the true reflection of what students are really learning and retaining will come through in the pages of

---

[1] Consider also the teacher's guide to this storybook, available through UAHC Press.
[2] Wiggins, Grant and Jay McTighe, *Understanding by Design*. Alexandria, VA: ASCD, 1998.

their personal (homework) journal *SEFER AVODAH* or *Avodah* Workbook. Although second-graders are at various ability levels when it comes to writing, the homework assigned in their *SEFER AVODAH* mostly requires simple sentence completion and allows students to answer either in writing or using artwork (drawings, image pasting, or other forms that might suit the students' levels and skills). The journal's centrality is that it provides students with an opportunity to reflect on what is being taught in class, to look back at what they experienced in class and bring home that learning, and to understand how the core of what they study builds up a connection between them and God.

Why Can't I See God?

Introduction

When discussing *avodah* as a means of connecting with God, the most difficult question we need to answer for our students is, "How can we connect with a being that we cannot see?"

Judaism teaches us that God should never be given anthropomorphic features (in language, art and other representations). Nevertheless, your students may think of God as a being with human features, because that is the easiest way for them to relate to the unknowable, indescribable, and invisible. In fact, this is also the way we often speak of God as adults. We are simply limited by our language and our understanding. Students are also aware that they do not see God. It is the teachers' task to make students aware of God's presence in the world.

There are tangible signs of God's handiwork within creation. Once students begin to connect with the notion of God as creator, they can start feeling and also seeing God's presence through the lens of God's creations.

Enduring Understanding

➤ *Avodah* is prayer, ceremonies, and celebrations. *Avodah* is the work we do to find sacred connections to God, community, and self.

Essential Questions

1. What can I do to connect to God?

2. What is the evidence that there is a God?

3. How do prayer, ceremonies, and celebrations affect my world?

Question to be Addressed

• How can I see God's imprint in the world and thereby recognize God's presence?

Evidence of Understanding

• Students will create a God-collage, which shows their understanding of God as the creator and reflects God's imprint in the world.

Materials Needed

- Construction paper, glue, scissors, magazines

- The story book *Hello, Hello, Are You There, God?* by Molly Cone (New York: UAHC Press, 1999)

ACTIVITY PLAN

I.   SET INDUCTION – SEEING LOVE

- Tell students that you are going to be talking about seeing the invisible today!

- Ask students if they know of anything that is invisible. Have them name a few things that they know exist but cannot be seen with the eyes (i.e. love, friendship).

- Ask: How can we "see" feelings? How do you "see" love in other people or in yourself—for example, the love of your mom or dad for you?

II.   ACTIVITIES

1. Read the story "The Fish That Looked for Water" from *Hello, Hello, Are You There, God?* by Molly Cone (p. 5)

2. After reading the story, discuss the following questions:

   - What was the fish in the story looking for?

   - Why did he want to know about water?

   - Why was the fish unable to find water?

   - What did the wise old fish tell the young fish about water?

   - What kinds of things are around us that we can't see with our eyes? (Answers may include: Wind, air, sounds, all sorts of feelings.)

   - Which things, although invisible to our eye, are necessary for us to survive (answers may include air, light, but also love or happiness)?

   - How do we know things are there even if we can't see them?

   - How do you see God?

   NOTE: It is important that as many students as possible express their opinion about this last question. The subsequent discussion greatly depends on the possible answers offered by the class.

3. Tell students that although we cannot see God, we can see God's imprint all around us.

4. Explain that an imprint is an impression or a trace left somewhere, like wet, muddy boot prints all over the house, or deer tracks in the snow.

5. Ask if they can think of other kinds of imprints.

6. Explain that as the Creator of the world, God has left an imprint in creation. Ask them what are God's "traces" in the world. [The beauty of a flower; the perfect way in which the ecosystem functions (for example, how the rain nourishes the earth, that allows the plants to grow, that feed the animals, that feed us, and so on); the wonderful difference between the species, people, and things (how no two leaves, or no two human beings are the same), and so on.]

7. Tell them they are going to look through magazines that show pictures of nature and the world around us.

Art Activity: Finding God's Imprint

1. Set magazines out for students to look at.

2. Each student should have a large piece of construction paper, and there should be scissors and glue at each table.

3. Explain that each of them will be creating a picture that shows God's imprint in the world. Students should look for pictures in the magazines that they feel represent God's imprint, then cut out the pictures and glue them onto their construction paper.

III.   CONCLUSION: SHARING COLLAGES

1. Ask students to share their pictures and explain to the rest of the class why they chose to include those particular images and how these reflect God's imprint in the world.

2. Ask the following: How are you different than the fish in the story? (Try to lead them to say that they are no longer like the fish in the story because their eyes have been opened—they are now able to see God's imprint in the world, which is the only way of seeing an otherwise invisible God.)

SEFER AVODAH: My Jewish Workbook

At Home

Tell students to think back to all the things discussed in class about "seeing" God in the world around us, and to complete the following sentence:

I see God's imprint in the world ...... (where? when?)

Shabbat Blessings

Introduction

Although we are expected to pray on Shabbat, and doing so is a very important part of this day's ritual, it is not prayer itself that distinguishes Shabbat from the rest of the weekdays. Shabbat is first and foremost a day of rest and spiritual uplift. We are told that Shabbat is a glimpse of the world to come, a taste of what paradise on earth could be. The way in which we can get that glimpse is through rest and reflection. The word "Shabbat" in Hebrew is formed by the root-letters *shin* (ש), *bet* (ב) and *tav* (ת), which together form the Hebrew word for "rest."

The observance of Shabbat involves two commandments: to **remember** (*zachor*) and to **observe** (*shamor*). In the Book of Exodus 20:8, we read that the fourth commandment is "Remember the Sabbath day and keep it holy." It is later explained that this is "because for six days, *Adonai* made the heavens and the earth, the sea and all that is in them, and on the seventh day, [God] **rested**; therefore, *Adonai* blessed the Sabbath day and sanctified it" (Exodus 20:11). By resting, we sanctify the seventh day and emulate God's example. Surely if God is not too busy to take a day off, neither are we! In Deuteronomy 5:15, when Moses reiterates the Ten Commandments, he states a second thing that we must do on Shabbat: "Remember that you were slaves in the land of Egypt, and *Adonai*, your God brought you forth from there with a mighty hand and with an outstretched arm; therefore *Adonai* your God commanded you to **observe** [*shamor*] the Sabbath day."

We can conclude that the *avodah* for Shabbat is not simply "not working," but rather making time for those activities to which we do not devote ourselves during the busy week. The prophet Isaiah tells us, "If you shall honor [Shabbat] without doing what you always do…you shall delight yourself in *Adonai*" (Isaiah 58:13–14).

Enduring Understanding

➤ *Avodah* is prayer, ceremonies, and celebrations. *Avodah* is the work we do to find sacred connections to God, community, and self.

Essential Questions

1. What can I do to connect to God?

2. What is the evidence that there is a God?

3. How do prayer, ceremonies, and celebrations affect my world?

Question to be Addressed

- What can we and our families do to make Shabbat different from every other day of the week?

- What can you refrain from doing on Shabbat to help you feel closer to God?

Evidence of Understanding

- Students will experience Shabbat at home with their family and share reflections and pictures of their celebration with the class. (In communities where there are families who may not feel comfortable with this assignment, you may want to host a class dinner at your congregation or ask families to invite one another and host this dinner at their houses.)

Materials Needed

- Shabbat blessings

- Letter to parents and Family Shabbat Journal (in the students' *SEFER AVODAH*)

- Parent resources

- Disposable cameras

- Foil

- Biscuit dough

- Flour

- A Shabbat story (See p. 116 for suggestions)

  Optional:

- Egg

- Sesame and or poppy seeds

- Pastry brushes

Suggested Class Reading

- Zwerin, Raymond A. and Audrey Friedman Marcus. *Shabbat Can Be*, ill. by Yuri Salzman. New York: UAHC Press, 1979.

- Cone, Molly. *Who Knows Ten*, ill. by Robin Brickman. New York: UAHC Press, 1998.

- Syme, Deborah Shayne. *Partners*, ill. by Jeffrey Wiener. New York: UAHC Press, 1989.

New Vocabulary

Shabbat	According to the Jewish calendar, the seventh day of the week, which starts on Friday at sundown and ends on Saturday at sundown. In English it is often referred to as "Sabbath." In Yiddish, an old dialect of Ashkenazi Jewry, Shabbat is usually pronounced "Shabbas" or "Shabbos."
challah	Traditional braided bread baked for Shabbat or Jewish holidays and festivals.
Havdalah	*lit.* "Separation" ceremony by which the end of Shabbat is celebrated and the new week is welcomed on Saturday evenings.
kadosh	Hebrew for "holy."
Kiddush	Blessing recited or chanted over wine, which emphasizes the holiness of Shabbat and festivals.
mitzvah (*pl.* mitzvot)	A commandment.
tzedakah box	Charity box in which *tzedakah* is collected, especially before Shabbat begins on Friday evening. The Yiddish word for a *tzedakah* box is *pushke*.

ACTIVITY PLAN

I.   SET INDUCTION

- Ask students to complete the following sentence previously written on the board:

   "If I could do the things I like the most for just one day, I would choose to…"

- Have students share their responses.

- Explain that in fact Judaism gives us this special day: it's Shabbat. On Shabbat we are supposed to stop doing what we normally (and routinely) do during the week and devote our-selves to something we truly enjoy but don't have time for on a regular day. The word "holy" means extra-ordinary (or "out of the ordinary") and Shabbat is meant to be a *holy* day, a day unlike every other day.

• Ask students:

Now we know that Judaism gives us the gift of this special *holy* day each week. What can you and your family do to make Shabbat holy, to make it extraordinary?

• Have students brainstorm a list of possible things or activities. You may want to include this list in the letter you send home to their parents.

II. LEARNING ACTIVITIES

Making Challah

1. Explain to students that one thing that makes Shabbat special is the special foods we eat. Ask them if they know of any food especially eaten on Shabbat. (Suggestions to get the ball rolling may include: challah, grape juice, chicken soup, gefilte fish, etc.) Explain that today the class will be making one of those special foods: challah.

2. After making sure that students have washed their hands, give each of them the following items:

   • a square of tin foil

   • three biscuits from a tin of Pillsbury-type ready-made biscuits from the refrigerator sec-tion of the grocery stores

   • a small pile of flour

3. Instruct students to take a biscuit and dip it in the flour with their hands, then roll each piece into a long snake and braid them together, pinching the dough at the top and bot-tom so that the braid is not left loose at either end.

4. To give the "class-made" challah an even more traditional look, students can lightly brush the loaf with egg white and sprinkle with poppy seeds or sesame seeds. Students can leave their challah on the tin foil and write their name on the foil in ink or permanent marker so they will be able to identify it later.

5. Individual challot should be placed onto cookie sheets and baked according to package directions. If you have enough funds, you may want to let each child bake two loaves, one to have for a snack and one to take home.

6. While the challot are baking, teach students the *Motzi*. Explain that this is the traditional Jewish blessing over bread (recited on Shabbat, although not exclusively).

7. Hand out copies of the *Motzi*. The teacher can also post it on the board. Read the blessing to the students. Have them repeat after you. Let those students who may already be familiar with the blessing lead their classmates. Give volunteer students an opportunity to practice.

Sharing a Shabbat Story

- To induce a sense of calm, quiet, and relaxation that the students should associate with Shabbat rest and peacefulness, the teacher can ask them to sit down comfortably on the floor, in a circle, and read them a story. Suggested readings include: *Shabbat Can Be* (particularly indicated for this lesson model); *Who Knows Ten*; or *Partners*.

- Make sure you leave time to enjoy the fresh baked challah together!

III. CONCLUSION

While everybody is eating the challot, ask each student to share one thing he or she looks forward to doing with the family on Shabbat. Alternatively, you may have each student write the thing they are most looking forward to at the bottom of the letter that is going home to their parents.

SEFER AVODAH: My Jewish Workbook

At Home: Celebrating Shabbat

Each week a different group of two or three students will take home a disposable camera and take photos of their families while celebrating Shabbat. Each family will be asked to complete a Shabbat Celebration Journal (as explained in the letter to the parents that the students will bring home), which will be shared with the class during the next lesson. The family journal sheets and family photos will later create a bulletin board or poster display in the class.

The teacher should make sure that the disposable cameras have a flash. If purchasing these cameras is not possible, then the homework will solely consist of the Shabbat Celebration Journal.

Parent Resources for Shabbat Celebration

Teachers: When preparing this list for your class, you may just want to list those books available in your congregational library.

1. Perelson, Ruth. *Invitation to Shabbat.* New York: UAHC Press, 1997. Everything you ever wanted to know about Shabbat in an accessible volume that assumes no prior knowledge.

2. Rauchwerger, Lisa. *Chocolate Chip Challah and Other Twists on the Jewish Holdiay Table.* New York: UAHC Press, 1999. This interactive cookbook for families is filled with a variety of delicious holiday treats, as well as information about the various holidays. It is designed for parents and children to use together.

3. Shapiro, Mark Dov. *Gates of Shabbat.* New York: CCAR Press, 1990. This book is a how-to, with answers to any questions you might have about the whys and hows of Jewish ritual and practice. Information on Friday night blessings can be found on pp. 14–32, 15, 20, 23-24, 27.

4. Olitzky, Kerry M. and Ronald H. Isaacs. *The How-to Handbook for Jewish Living.* Hoboken, N.J.: KTAV Publishing House, 1993. A step-by-step guide with text references and additional recommended resources.

5. *Do It Yourself Shabbat.* Prepared by the Family Education Committee of the UAHC-CCAR Commission on Jewish Education. This is a handy, fold-out, washable card written with both traditional and single-parent households in mind. http://uahc.org/educate/

6. Zwerin, Raymond A. and Marcus Audrey Friedman. *Shabbat Can Be.* New York: UAHC Press, 1979. A wonderful, warm story about exactly what this lessons hopes families will do!

Internet resources:

http://www.jewish.com/holidays/shabbat.shtml—Basic holiday information.

http://judaism.about.com/culture/religion/jud—Basic holiday information.

http://uahc.org/clickonj/pages/shabbat02.htm—An article on just where to start when introducing Shabbat celebration in your home.

http://uahc.org/shabbat/index.shtml—"Shabbat Family Table Talk." Family discussion suggestions for the weekly Torah portion.

Date _____

Dear Parents:

Our last lesson was centered on Shabbat. We explored how celebrating Shabbat by doing something really special, that we don't have time to do during the week, is a way of making Shabbat truly holy and it is part of avodah-the work of the heart to find sacred connections to God, community, and self. We would appreciate it if your family could take a moment to sit down together and complete the Shabbat Celebration Journal over the next few weeks.

In class we discussed the teaching of the prophet Isaiah, who said that celebrating Shabbat means to take time out from the ordinary. So, next Shabbat, we invite you to do something different that you don't do every day-whether it's lighting candles at the dinner table on Friday night, saying blessings together, attending synagogue, or cooking a special dish that you all enjoy. Students came up with several different suggestions for what they think could make their Shabbat "special"; don't forget to ask your child(ren) to share with you the list of ideas generated in class. In addition, students learned the Motzi blessings for Erev Shabbat (Friday night).

We are including several resources that might help you with your home Shabbat celebrations: blessings in Hebrew, English, and transliteration, and a resource sheet which lists websites and books for you and your child(ren). We hope that you will find celebrating Shabbat an enjoyable family activity, and we look forward to hearing about and learning from your experience.

Sincerely,

_____

My Family Shabbat Journal

Please complete the journal together. You may choose to answer in writing or by drawing pictures.

This week we celebrated Shabbat by...

- We did these special activities_____

_____

_____

- We ate these special foods_____

_____

_____

- The day felt special because_____

_____

_____

- We felt close to God when/because_____

_____

_____

Shabbat Blessings

For the candles

בָּרוּךְ אַתָּה יְיָ אֱלֹהֵינוּ מֶלֶךְ הָעוֹלָם, אֲשֶׁר
קִדְּשָׁנוּ בְּמִצְוֹתָיו, וְצִוָּנוּ לְהַדְלִיק נֵר שֶׁל שַׁבָּת.

Baruch atah Adonai, Eloheinu Melech haolam, asher kid'shanu
b'mitzvotav v'tzivanu l'hadlik ner shel Shabbat.

Blessed are You, *Adonai* our God, Ruler of the Universe, who sanctifies us by
Your commandments and commands us to kindle the lights of Shabbat.

For the wine

בָּרוּךְ אַתָּה יְיָ אֱלֹהֵינוּ מֶלֶךְ הָעוֹלָם, בּוֹרֵא פְּרִי הַגָּפֶן.

Baruch atah Adonai, Eloheinu Melech haolam, borei p'ri hagafen.

Blessed are You, *Adonai* our God, Ruler of the Universe, who creates the fruit of the vine.

For the challah

בָּרוּךְ אַתָּה יְיָ אֱלֹהֵינוּ מֶלֶךְ הָעוֹלָם, הַמּוֹצִיא לֶחֶם מִן הָאָרֶץ.

Baruch atah Adonai, Eloheinu Melech haolam, hamotzi lechem min ha-aretz.

Blessed are You, *Adonai* our God, Ruler of the Universe,
who brings forth bread from the earth.

MOTZI: WE THANK GOD FOR THE GIFT OF BREAD...

 **Morning Blessings**

Introduction

The traditional Jewish morning prayer is known as the *Modeh Ani*. Part of our *avodah*, the work of the heart to connect to God, is also making time in the morning, as soon as we wake up, to think of the new day ahead we are granted to live. It is a special time we take out of what is going to be our usual busy day to thank God for our life and for the beautiful things in it. *Modeh Ani* reminds us that the ability to wake up each morning renewed and refreshed, ready for a new day of life, is, indeed, a gift.

Enduring Understanding

➤ *Avodah* is prayer, ceremonies, and celebrations. *Avodah* is the work we do to find sacred connections to God, community, and self.

Essential Questions

1. What can I do to connect to God?

2. What is the evidence that there is a God?

3. How do prayer, ceremonies, and celebrations affect my world?

Questions to be Addressed

- How is each new day a gift from God?

- How can we say thanks for this gift?

- How can we show gratitude to God for our lives?

Evidence of Understanding

- Students will be able to complete the sentence: "On this new day I am thankful to God because…"

Materials Needed

- Acrostic poem handouts

- *Modeh Ani* prayer handouts

- Note to parents about the students' *SEFER AVODAH*

- White construction paper (recommended 12x16-inch sheets)

- Watercolors

- Paintbrushes

- Cups for the watercolor paints

- Glue

- CD player and music from the following CDs:

    Black, Joe. *Aleph Bet Boogie.* Albuquerque, NM: Lanitunes Music, 1991.

    Kol B'seder. *Songs for Growin'—Music for Jewish Families.* New York: Transcontinental Music/UAHC, 2001.

    Good Morning, Good Night—Jewish Children's Songs for Daytime and Bedtime. New York: Transcontinental Music Publications, 2001

Reading Resources for Teachers

- UAHC website: www.uahc.org/educate/wakeup

- Abromowitz, Yosef and Susan Silverman. *Jewish Family Life: Traditions, Holidays, and Values for Today's Parents and Children.* New York: Golden Books, 1997. Or visit the website: www.jewishfamily.com.

New Vocabulary

Modeh Ani	*lit.* "I give thanks." Opening words of the Hebrew morning prayer to be recited upon awakening
Modeh ani l'fanecha Melech chai v'kayam shehechezarta bi nishmati b'chemlah; rabah emunatecha.	"I give thanks to You, O God, eternal and living Ruler, Who in mercy has returned my soul to me; great is your faithfuness."

ACTIVITY PLAN

I. SET INDUCTION: WAKING UP

- Ask students to pantomime what they do each morning as they wake up. Do they stretch, climb out of bed, or snuggle back under the covers? What do they do when they get out of bed?

- After each student had a chance to act out his or her morning awakening, ask them to answer the following questions:

  What does your body feel like in the morning?

  What's exciting about beginning a new day?

- Explain to the students that according to Judaism each new day is a gift that we should be thankful for, an opportunity to improve yourself and our world.

II. LEARNING ACTIVITIES

Being Thankful—An Acrostic Poem

1. Explain to students that they will be learning the traditional blessing upon beginning a new day. Tell students that one act of *avodah* is giving thanks to God, especially for our lives each new day, and also for the many things that make our lives wonderful.

2. Ask students to think quietly about things in their life they are thankful for. Then give each student the acrostic poem worksheet (see p. 128).

3. Tell students that thinking about this list each morning as they wake up will help them remember to give thanks to God.

Creating Morning Frames for the Poems

1. Give each student a piece of white construction paper.

2. Tell them to think about what they see when they wake up each morning.

3. Explain that they will paint a watercolor picture that will be a frame for their God-thanking poems.

4. Pass out paints and paintbrushes.

Learning *Modeh Ani*

1. While the pictures are drying, the teacher can engage the class in reading and learning the *Modeh Ani* prayer, which should have been posted on the board beforehand.

2. Read the blessing for the students, then have them repeat the words after you. Ask them to read the sentence aloud again. Let those students who may already be familiar with the blessing lead their classmates.

3. Ask if there is anybody who would like to try to read the sentence aloud alone. Give as many students as possible an opportunity to practice.

   NOTE: There are several nice melodies to accompany this prayer. The teacher may want to invite the cantor or music teacher to sing or play them, or bring in tapes for the students to listen to the songs.

III.   CONCLUSION

1. Have students glue their poems onto the frames. Words to *Modeh Ani* should also be glued onto the pictures to prompt them each morning.

2. Those who wish to do so may share their poems with the rest of the class.

3. Hand out copies of the letter for the students' parents.

4. Explain the homework. Underline that it is important to involve parents in this home activity: Students should have their parents help them find a good place to hang their poems, so that they are visible every morning when the students wake up.

Sefer Avodah: My Jewish Workbook

At Home

Think about what you have learned in class today: the importance of connecting to God at the very start of each day, when we wake up in the morning. According to Judaism, thanking God for the new day we are given is part of *avodah*, the work of the heart we do to find sacred connections to God.

Thinking about the things you can be happy and thankful for when you wake up in the morning, complete the following open sentence:

On this new day I am thankful to God because…

Repeat this exercise at least **three times** before our next class.

Date _____

Dear Parents:

As part of our ongoing learning about avodah, the "work" we do to find sacred connections to God, community, and self, today we have studied in class the blessing Modeh Ani. These two Hebrew words (that literally mean "I give thanks") open the traditional morning prayer we recite to thank God for the new day of life we are given to experience. It is the Jewish way of taking the time to stop and connect to God just before the busy routine of our daily lives sets in and grabs all our attention and strength. Students have written and decorated beautiful poems about expressing gratefulness to God that will help them remember to thank God each morning.

Over the next week, we hope that you will try to say this blessing with your child(ren). Students have also been assigned the homework of completing the sentence "On this new day I am thankful to God because..." at least three times during the coming week. Remind your child(ren) to do the assignment and bring it to the next class. You may want to add your own thoughts to this journal (SEFER AVODAH) as well. We would love to hear them. It would probably help if your child kept his or her SEFER AVODAH by the bed, so that completing the sentence and thinking of God at the start of every new day will become a ritual.

Thank you for your participation.

Sincerely,

_____

Acrostic Poem Worksheet

Take a few minutes to think about the things in your life for which you are thankful. Fill in the spaces below with the names of things you are grateful to God for that start with the same letters that make up the word "THANKFUL" (for example, *T* as in "Tree": I am thankful to God for the beautiful trees in the parks and forests). This is called an acrostic poem; there are many examples of poems like this in our Bible and in our prayers.

I am

T_____

H_____

A_____

N_____

K_____

F_____

U_____

L_____

To God

_____
Your Name

מוֹדֶה אֲנִי לְפָנֶיךָ, מֶלֶךְ חַי וְקַיָּם, שֶׁהֶחֱזַרְתָּ בִּי נִשְׁמָתִי בְּחֶמְלָה רַבָּה אֱמוּנָתֶךָ.

Modeh ani l'fanecha Melech chai v'kayam shehechezarta bi nish-mati b'chemlah; rabah emunatecha.

I give thanks to You, O God, eternal and living Ruler,

Who in mercy has returned my soul to me;

great is Your faithfulness.

Sh'ma

Introduction

It is often a struggle for students to understand how being Jewish makes them different. This lesson will explain the root and significance of this "Jewish uniqueness" as epitomized by the central Jewish declaration of faith: the *Sh'ma*. Our unique destiny begins when Abraham understands, believes, and articulates (for the first time in our history) that the world is created by the One and only God. It is our continued affirmation of this belief in our daily worship that helps us maintain our unique destiny. By saying the words, "Hear O Israel, *Adonai* Is Our God, *Adonai* Is One," we connect to God and to generations of Jews who declared their belief in God and God's oneness.

The *Sh'ma* is the oldest daily prayer in Judaism and was probably part of the service at the time of the First Temple. Jewish law requires that the *Sh'ma* be said twice daily: once in the morning and once after dark. According to Jewish tradition, it is customary to recite this prayer two additional times during the day: before going to bed at night, and during the preliminary prayer service preceding the regular morning prayer service.[1]

This is intended to be the first of a two-part lesson. The second part will center on the "Evening Blessings." The core activity for these lessons is a long art project that will require about two weeks to complete. It is important to bring students' attention to the fact that this prayer is so important, so central in Judaism, that it is the only one to deserve a two-week-long activity.

Enduring Understanding

> *Avodah* is prayer, ceremonies, and celebrations. *Avodah* is the work we do to find sacred connections to God, community, and self.

---

[1] Lamm, Norman. *The Shema: Spirituality and Law in Judaism*. Philadelphia: The Jewish Publication Society, 1998; p.5.

Essential Questions

1. How does the *Sh'ma* set us apart as a people?

2. How does using different modalities for prayer help worshippers connect to the words and to the Divine?

Evidence of Understanding

- Students will be able to recite the *Sh'ma*.

- Students will be able to complete the sentence: When I listen to God, I hear...

Materials Needed

- *Sh'ma* blessing sheets

- "Reflecting on the *Sh'ma*" sheet to compare different experiences related to saying the *Sh'ma*

- Pencils

- Plain white paper

- Handkerchiefs

- Fabric markers and/or puffy paints

- *Sh'ma* tracing sheets

- Homework reminder

Useful Resources

- The full text of the *Sh'ma* prayer, in Hebrew, English, and transliteration, along with a MIDI file of the tune, can be found online at www.jewfaq.org/prayer/Sh'ma.

New Vocabulary

Adonai	Hebrew word for God
Sh'ma	*lit.* "Hear!" The first word of the *Sh'ma* prayer

ACTIVITY PLAN

II. SET INDUCTION

1. Ask students to sit in a comfortable position (space allowing, they can even lie down on the floor).

2. Turn the lights out and ask students to close their eyes, not say a word, and simply listen to the silence. In order to have students focus and keep as quiet as possible, it might be useful to tell them to breathe and concentrate on (listen to) their breathing.

3. After the class has remained silent and relaxed for a few minutes, ask the following questions:

   What did you hear?

   Did you notice any new sounds in the classroom you had never heard before?

   Why were you able to hear new sounds?

4. Ask how having their eyes closed affected the listening experience (Did it help? Why?).

5. Explain to the students that they are going to learn to "listen" to God today. Tell them that Judaism gives us a special prayer that helps us do that. This prayer is called the *Sh'ma* (which means "listen" or "hear"), the most important prayer of the Jewish people.

II. LEARNING ACTIVITIES

Saying the *Sh'ma*

1. The teacher can post the *Sh'ma* on the board and hand out a copy to each student. (See p. 135)

2. Read the blessing to the students in Hebrew and English. Then, have them repeat after you. Let those students who might be familiar with the blessing lead their classmates. Give students an opportunity to practice.

Hearing *Sh'ma* and Reflecting

1. Tell students that saying a prayer requires concentration. A person has to mean the words he or she is reciting and in order to understand and "feel" those words, one should intensely focus on the prayer. Explain that reciting a prayer in different ways may help the worshipper concentrate better.

2. Explain that the *Sh'ma* is considered the most important prayer for the Jews, because it reminds us of what makes us unique: Our belief in one God. The *Sh'ma* also reminds us that we are special to God, and we are expected to listen to God. When we listen to God's words, we are able to communicate with God and hear God "speak" to us in different ways.

3. Explain to them that today, by reciting the *Sh'ma* in several different ways, each student will discover his or her most effective way of concentrating to hear God.

4. Hand out "Reflecting on the *Sh'ma*" sheet and pencils.

5. Explain to students that they will have a few minutes after each time the *Sh'ma* is recited to complete their thoughts.

6. Read the instructions and the chart to ensure that students understand.

7. Say the *Sh'ma* in five different ways:

   • Saying *Sh'ma* with my eyes open

   • Saying *Sh'ma* with my eyes closed

   • Saying *Sh'ma* with my name

   NOTE: Students will substitute the word "Israel" with their own name. Depending on the comprehension level of the class, the teacher could try to explain the following: the *Sh'ma* is a prayer that calls for all of Israel (i.e., all the Jews) to hear God's words; but Yisrael is also the new name that God gave to our forefather Jacob. So the *Sh'ma* is both a collective prayer for the entire community of Jews, and a personal prayer for each single Jew. By substituting the name of Jacob/Yisrael with our birth names, each student may feel the "call" of the *Sh'ma* as a personal call to hear what God has to say to him or her.

   • Singing *Sh'ma:* Use any melody for the *Sh'ma* and play it for the students, or invite your cantor or music teacher to perform the *Sh'ma* songs in class.

   • Signing *Sh'ma* (you can teach students or simply show them how it is possible to say the *Sh'ma* "without words"—there are numerous resources available from public libraries and on specialized websites on the internet with instructions on how to recite the *Sh'ma* using sign language)

Making *Sh'ma* Pillow Covering

1. Explain that this prayer is so important for the Jews the class will be spending two weeks learning about it and working on a special project which will always remind them of the *Sh'ma*. The project will be a special handkerchief "pillow cover." When finished, it can be attached to a pillowcase or wrapped around a favorite stuffed animal.

2. Give each student a handkerchief, a *Sh'ma* tracing sheet, pencil, and blank sheet of paper. Explain that they will be writing the *Sh'ma* on their handkerchief. They may trace the Hebrew, write it on their own, or choose just to put the English on.

3. Suggest to students that they might want to plan their design on the paper before they do it on the handkerchief. Also, doing the design in pencil first will make decorating easier. Try to use aprons, or let parents know beforehand you will be doing an art project. Students should dress appropriately, since fabric markers and puffy paint often stain. This is a good project in which to invite parents to take part! Even just a few extra hands will greatly help the teacher.

4. Set out the fabric markers and puffy paints for students to write their *Sh'ma*. Plan to complete the writing of the *Sh'ma* at this class.

5. For a beautiful background, begin a week earlier and tie-dye the handkerchiefs.

6. After students finish this part of the project, assign and explain the homework in their *SEFER AVODAH*.

III. CONCLUSIONS

• Give each student a chance to share with the class his or her favorite way to say the *Sh'ma* as indicated in his or her chart.

• Ask students to share their *Sh'ma* reflection charts with their parents at home.

SEFER AVODAH: My Jewish Workbook

• Ask students to complete the following sentence:

"When I listen to God, I hear…"

• Invite students to recite the *Sh'ma* at night, just before going to bed. They should try to do this over the next few days before the following class.

Sh'ma Blessing

שְׁמַע יִשְׂרָאֵל יְיָ אֱלֹהֵינוּ יְיָ אֶחָד:

Sh'ma Yisrael Adonai Eloheinu Adonai Echad

Hear, Israel, *Adonai* is our God, *Adonai* is One.

בָּרוּךְ שֵׁם כְּבוֹד מַלְכוּתוֹ לְעוֹלָם וָעֶד.

Baruch Shem k'vod malchuto l'olam va-ed

Blessed is God's glorious kingdom for ever and ever.

Reflecting on Sh'ma

As you listen and say the *Sh'ma* in different ways, think about how each way makes you feel. Check the box that expresses how you feel.

♥   Which is your favorite way to say *Sh'ma?* Put a heart in that row.

✱   Which way makes it easiest for you to listen to God? Put a star in that row.

WAYS OF LISTENING	Helps me pay attention	Makes me feel happy	Makes me feel warm inside	Makes me feel calm	Helps me hear God
Saying *Sh'ma* with my eyes open					
Saying *Sh'ma* with my eyes closed					
Saying *Sh'ma* with my name					
Singing *Sh'ma*					
Signing *Sh'ma*					

Homework Reminder

(In *SEFER AVODAH*)

Please share this sheet with your parents and tell them what we learned about the *Sh'ma*, our most important Jewish prayer. Put this sheet by your bed during the week and try to recite the prayer at least once before you go to bed. Think about how saying this prayer makes you feel at night. Write down your thoughts to bring with you next week and share with the class if you want.

שְׁמַע יִשְׂרָאֵל יְיָ אֱלֹהֵינוּ יְיָ אֶחָד:

Sh'ma Yisrael Adonai Eloheinu Adonai Echad

Hear, Israel, *Adonai* is our God, *Adonai* is One.

בָּרוּךְ שֵׁם כְּבוֹד מַלְכוּתוֹ לְעוֹלָם וָעֶד.

Baruch Shem k'vod malchuto l'olam va-ed

Blessed is God's glorious kingdom for ever and ever.

THOUGHTS FOR NEXT WEEK'S CLASS:

When I said the *Sh'ma* at night I felt ...

When I listened for God, I could hear ...

Sh'ma Tracing

שְׁמַע יִשְׂרָאֵל יְיָ אֱלֹהֵינוּ יְיָ אֶחָד׃

Hear, Israel, Adonai is our God, Adonai is One.

Evening Blessings

Introduction

As teachers, we know how important ritual and routine are for a classroom. This is also true of a student's life at home. Rituals, and especially Jewish rituals, provide a sense of comfort and connection. Among them are traditional evening blessings (special prayers at the end of the day that allow us to reflect and meditate) and petitionary prayers (in which we ask God to watch over us as we sleep).

As discussed in the previous lesson, the *Sh'ma* has been the Jewish declaration of faith for thousands of years. Jews everywhere say the *Sh'ma* at night to remind themselves of the connection to the One God. By turning our thoughts toward God and repeating ancient words of our tradition, we transform daily bedtime into universal Jewish time. This helps our students understand that being Jewish is a way of life, something we do inside and outside the synagogue walls and especially within the walls of our homes.

Enduring Understanding

➤ *Avodah* is prayer, ceremonies, and celebrations. *Avodah* is the work we do to find sacred connections to God, community, and self.

Essential Questions

1. What can I do to connect to God?

2. What is the evidence that there is a God?

3. How do prayer, ceremonies, and celebrations affect my world?

Question to be Addressed

• How can the words of the *Sh'ma* provide comfort and reflective time at night?

Evidence of Understanding

- Students will complete their *Sh'ma* pillow cover from last week with comforting thoughts to make them feel safe and watched over at night.

Materials Needed

- Handkerchiefs worked on during the previous lesson

- Handkerchiefs with the words of the *Sh'ma* prepared by the teacher for those students who weren't at the previous lesson

- Plain white paper and pencils

- Fabric markers and/or puffy paint

- Ribbons, buttons, sequins, anything for decorating

- Tacky glue

- Journal sheets

- Letters for the parents

Useful Resources

- http://uahc.org/press/bedtime/index.html

- *On the Doorposts of Your House—Prayers and Ceremonies for the Jewish Home.* Chaim Stern, ed. New York: CCAR Press, 1994.

ACTIVITY PLAN

I. SET INDUCTION

1. Begin by reflecting on the learning and conclusions from the previous lesson.

2. Ask students who remembered to say the *Sh'ma* before going to bed at least once during the past week. (If anyone completed the sentences assigned in their *SEFER AVODAH*, and if students want to, have them share their reflections on how it felt saying the *Sh'ma* before falling asleep.) Ask:

    How did it feel to say the *Sh'ma* at night?

What did you hear as you said the *Sh'ma* and paid attention to its words?

Did you feel differently about going to bed after saying the *Sh'ma*? Why/how?

3. Practice saying the *Sh'ma* together for review.

II. LEARNING ACTIVITIES

Comforting Our Nights and Our Sleep: The *Sh'ma*

1. Explain to students that many Jews say the *Sh'ma* each night before they go to bed. Its words are meant to bring comfort, and help to reflect on the day just passed, before we fall asleep.

2. Ask students what they do at night to get ready for bed.

3. Ask students what things, among the many they do during the day, make them feel happy and proud of themselves at night before going to bed. What images or thoughts are good and comforting and make them feel safe and happy when they go to bed? Brainstorm a list on the board.

4. Ask students to sit or even lie down in very comfortable positions, as if they were in their beds. Tell them to imagine they are home, it's night and they are getting ready to sleep. Ask them to close their eyes and recite the *Sh'ma* together.

5. How can saying the *Sh'ma* help them sleep better? (Answers may include: by making us feel connected to God; by reminding us we are part of a people; by turning our thoughts to the positive.)

Sh'ma Pillow Cover (Part II)

1. Hand back projects from the previous week. Students who were not present at the last class can use the handkerchiefs with the words of the *Sh'ma* on them prepared beforehand by teacher.

2. Hand out pencils and white paper. Ask students to think about decorating their *Sh'ma* pillow covers and explain how they might use them at night. Tell students to look at the list on the board and think of comforting images that will help them sleep at night.

3. Set out the sequins, ribbons, and other decorations in small bowls at each table. Make sure there is also glue at each table.

4. As students complete their projects, show them the journal pages in their *SEFER AVODAH* for them to complete.

III.   CONCLUSIONS

Before class is over, draw everyone into a circle and have students share a little bit about their pillow covers and why they decorated them the way they did. Ask each student to share his or her answers to the journal question, "Saying the *Sh'ma* at night will make me feel...because..." Remember to hand out the letters for the parents.

SEFER AVODAH: My Jewish Workbook

Ask students to complete the two parts of the following sentence:

Saying the *Sh'ma* at night will make me feel... because...

Date _____

Dear Parents:

During our previous lesson, we studied the words to the most important prayer of the Jewish people, the Sh'ma. Students had been asked to share with you some of the things learned in class about the Sh'ma: our uniqueness as a people, and our ability to feel close to God when we recite this prayer and pay attention to its words. We hope that you saw the homework and that your child shared some of these ideas with you last week.

Today your child(ren) brought home a Sh'ma pillow cover. We have worked on this special project for two weeks. It would be ideal if students could attach this cover to a special pillowcase, or even wrap it around a special stuffed animal, so that they can keep it close each night as they sleep.

We spent the last two lessons talking about the Sh'ma and its centrality in our belief. We learned how to say this prayer with deep concentration in order to be able to hear God-each of us in his or her own special way. We spent a great deal of time on this art project, trying to think of pictures and colors that would make each student feel warm and safe at night. Jews everywhere recite the Sh'ma at night to remind themselves of the connection to the One God. By turning our thoughts toward God and repeating ancient words of our tradition, we transform ordinary bedtime into special Jewish time, thus helping children understand that being Jewish is a way of life, something we do inside and outside the synagogue and especially within the walls of our homes. We hope that this art project will inspire you and your children to say this prayer each night before you go to bed.

Thank you for your interest and participation in your child(ren)'s Jewish learning.

Sincerely,

_____

How Do I Talk to God?

Introduction

As expressed by the title, this lesson will address the question of *how* we communicate with God. The text used for this lesson tells the story of a young boy who, not knowing Hebrew, expresses his prayers to God playing the flute—for which he has a special talent. The significant teaching to be drawn from this lesson is that ultimately each of us will find our own way of communicating with God, whether it is through a particular talent, through our own spoken words, or through the traditional Hebrew prayers of our people. Our Enduring Understanding reminds us that *avodah* is the way we, as individuals as well as a community, find our own sacred connection to God.

Our tradition has considered prayer the primary means of communication with God ever since the destruction of the Second Temple. Even before that time, there were fixed prayers that Jews would recite when offering a sacrifice (an important religious custom used to communicate with God in ancient times). But it is not until the sixth century that the prayer service is organized in a fixed order called *keva*—one half of the worship experience. We are also taught that we cannot consider our prayers truly complete unless we have added the words of our hearts to the words of our tradition. The great task of a teacher is to help students find the "words of the heart" and their own special ways of expressing them.

Enduring Understanding

> *Avodah* is prayer, ceremonies, and celebrations. *Avodah* is the work we do to find sacred connections to God, community, and self.

Essential Questions

1. What can I do to connect to God?

2. What is the evidence that there is a God?

3. How do prayer, ceremonies, and celebrations affect my world?

Question to be Addressed

- How can I feel comfortable communicating with God?

Evidence of Understanding

- Student will create a personal prayer of thanks to God, in writing or using art forms.

Materials Needed

- Tape recorder

- The song "Thank You God" from the tape/CD *It's So Amazing*, by Doug Cotler (Denver, CO: A.R.E. Publishing, 2000)

- Markers, paper, crayons

- Blank audiotapes for recording

- "The Boy and the Flute" from *Hello, Hello, Are You There God?*, by Molly Cone (pp. 7–8).

New Vocabulary

Baruch atah Adonai, Eloheinu Melech haolam

lit. "Blessed are you, *Adonai* our God, Ruler of the world." Opening sentence of many Jewish prayers in Hebrew. *Baruch* [Blessed] *atah* [you] *Adonai* [My Lord; mostly used in Hebrew], *Eloheinu* [Our God] *Melech* [King; Ruler] *haolam* [of the world]

ACTIVITY PLAN

I. SET INDUCTION

1. Have the sentence "*Baruch atah Adonai, Eloheinu Melech haolam*—Thank you God …" written on the board when students walk in.

2. Explain that today we are going to be talking about things in our lives for which we should be thankful. Ask each student to share one thing for which he or she is grateful to God.

3. Teach them Doug Cotler's song, "Thank You God" (lyrics can be found in the tape or CD, in the words available from the tape cover, or in the songbook *The Doug Cotler Songbook II*, also available from A.R.E. Publishing).

4. Explain that in the Jewish tradition we have blessings to say "Thank You" to God and to ask for special things. Traditionally all blessings begin with the same six words: *Baruch atah, Adonai, Eloheinu Melech haolam.* Pronounce these words for the students and have the class repeat them so that all can learn the phrase.

5. Ask students how they say "Thank You" to God, and how someone who doesn't know these Hebrew words or the Hebrew prayers can say, "Thank You, God."

II.   Learning Activities

1. Read and discuss the story "The Boy and the Flute."

2. Ask the following questions and discuss:

   What was the boy's special gift?

   What songs could the boy play?

   Did the boy know how to pray?

   What happened when the people in the congregation heard the boy's flute?

   What did the rabbi say about the boy's prayer?

3. Ask students if they know any prayers, and if so to share them with the rest of the class. (Perhaps they might be familiar with a holiday blessing, or a Shabbat blessing.)

4. Tell students to think back to what they shared at the opening circle. What is the best way to say, "Thank you, God"?

5. Explain that each student is going to have a chance to create his or her own prayer. They may choose to write one or draw a picture that represents the meaning of their prayer. Remind them about the six opening words of the Hebrew blessings which they have learned, and that might be used now in their composition or drawing.

Creating the Prayers

1. Explain to students that they will have the same opportunity the boy with the flute had: a chance to create their own special blessing to thank God.

2. Have supplies set out at each table: blessing sheets, markers, crayons, pencils. Tell students to take a few quiet minutes to think about what they want to say to God before they begin creating their prayer.

III. CONCLUSION

1. Bring the students together in a circle on the floor. Try to create a sense of intimate space.

2. Have each student share his or her prayer by reading it, describing it, singing, or whatever other means they chose to express themselves.

3. Sing all together the song "Thank You God" one more time and have students hold up their pictures during the singing.

SEFER AVODAH: My Jewish Workbook

Blessing Sheet

Instruct students to open their *SEFER AVODAH* journal, and explain the following:

1. In class you thought of some things you are thankful to God for. How can you say, "Thank you, God," for those good things in your life?

2. Remember how the boy in the story we read in class used his skills to say thanks to God. Take time to think of your own way to best thank God. You can put it in writing, or create an artwork or drawing that represents your thankfulness. Don't forget the six Hebrew words you learned in class—they might come in handy now if you choose to write your personal "thank you" note to God for the good things in your life.

I Thank God

בָּרוּךְ אַתָּה יְיָ אֱלֹהֵינוּ מֶלֶךְ הָעוֹלָם

Baruch atah Adonai, Eloheinu Melech haoam

Blessed are you, *Adonai* our God, Ruler of the Universe

Thank You God

Why Does God Want Me to Grow?

Introduction

As we teach about mitzvot (commandments) and *tikkun olam* (repairing the world) students often struggle with feelings of inadequacy, with the impression that there is not much they can do, being so young and so small, to make a difference in the world. Tradition teaches us that we are each obligated to do what we can to help repair the world, but that the full responsibility does not lie on any of us. In *Pirkei Avot* 2:16 we read: "You are not required to complete the work, neither are you free to avoid it."

As we grow, our minds grow in understanding and our bodies grow in ability. When we can use our minds and our bodies to help others, we become like God. As we grow older we learn about and take part in more and more mitzvot, we become more and more like God. God gives our bodies and minds the capacity for growth each day so that we can strive to make the world a better place.

Enduring Understanding

➤ *Avodah* is prayer, ceremonies, and celebrations. *Avodah* is the work we do to find sacred connections to God, community, and self.

Essential Questions

1. What can I do to connect to God?

2. What is the evidence that there is a God?

3. How do prayer, ceremonies, and celebrations affect my world?

Questions to be Addressed

1. How am I becoming more self–sufficient each day? What shows that I grow every day?

2. What can I do each day to make the world a better place? How can I contribute to *tikkun olam*?

Lesson Preparation

To be able to conduct this lesson, teachers need to write a letter to the parents asking them to send in photos and comments necessary for one of this unit's activities. See attached sample on page 154.

Evidence of Understanding

• Students will share ways in which they can help others, and their understanding of how helping others helps us feel good about ourselves.

• Students will be able to identify ways in which God has helped them grow, physically, intellectually, and spiritually.

Materials Needed

• Copies of the story "The Father," by Molly Cone, from *Hello, Hello, Are You There, God?* (New York: UAHC Press, 1999), pp. 14–15

• Markers

• Scissors

• Construction paper for frames

• Tape

• Glue

• Polaroid camera and film

New Vocabulary

tikkun olam   *lit.* "repairing the world." According to Rabbi Isaac Luria, a sixteenth-century kabbalist, the world broke during the act of creation, and each of us has a responsibility to help God to bring about wholeness in the world.

ACTIVITY PLAN

I. SET INDUCTION

1. As students enter the classroom, take a picture of them with a Polaroid camera and collect the baby pictures they should be bringing for this lesson. Tell students that they should pose for the picture showing something they are good at (like hitting a baseball, dancing, or drawing). Students can hold on to these for sharing later. (If the school does not own a Polaroid camera, the teacher may be able to borrow one from a parent, or simply have students draw self-portraits.)

2. When all the students have arrived, seat them in a circle.

3. Pass around the baby pictures that parents should have given the students to bring to class. Ask students to describe the pictures and what the babies are doing in them (all students can comment and talk; it is not necessary for each student to describe exclusively his or her own photo).

4. Make sure that each student gets his or her baby picture. Have them compare the baby pictures to their current pictures (taken earlier, before the lesson started):

    How are these two photos different? How are they similar?

    How would you describe the changes in the person portrayed in these pictures?

    What things couldn't the baby in the baby picture do that the same older boy or girl can do today?

    -Physically: (i.e., running, jumping, playing ball, etc.)

    -Intellectually: (i.e., reading, writing, coloring, understanding a movie)

    -Spiritually: (helping others, thinking about God)

5. Some parents may have included captions or reflections on the back. Share these with the students. Explain to students that when we grow and learn to take care of ourselves, our parents are proud of us.

II. Learning Activities

1. Read and discuss the story "The Father." Ask the following questions:

    What did the king want to know when he returned home?

    Was the king happy with how the servants had cared for his son?

How did the king help the prince?

How do you think the king felt when his son learned to walk?

2. Explain to students that just as the king wanted his son to learn to take care of himself, God wants us to grow and learn to take care of ourselves. When we grow through God's daily gift of life, we are doing what God wants. As our bodies grow, we can be more like God by helping others.

Bulletin Board: I am Growing—I am Doing My Part

1. Explain to students that they will be creating a bulletin board for their classroom, which shows how they are growing up and how they are learning to help one another.

2. Give each student a piece of construction paper to use as a frame for his or her pictures. Have students decorate the frame by writing on it how they have grown since they were babies. You may want to pre-print on the construction paper the sentence:

"I'm not a baby anymore, now I can…"

Or write it on the board and have students complete it. They may also want to simply decorate their frames. Comments written by parents should be cut and pasted onto the frame as well, or can go under the picture on the bulletin board.

3. Let students place their pictures on a bulletin board that reads, "I am growing—I am doing my part." In the center of the bulletin board should be a large picture of the Earth.

4. Ask students if they have seen anything in the world they think needs fixing. Give examples: people who are hungry, forest fires destroying national parks, etc. Explain that our world does need fixing and each of us has a responsibility, given by God, to do our part to help fix the world. This responsibility is called *tikkun olam*, repairing the world. When we do things to bring wholeness to the world we are acting as God's partner.

5. Post a sign that says "*Tikkun Olam*–Repairing the World–Being God's Partner" on the bulletin board.

6. Ask students what they can do to be God's partner; brainstorm a list on the board. Explain that many of the things they list are things they were not able to do when they were babies.

7. Give each student another piece of construction paper. Have them trace their hand and cut it out. Have students write in one finger one thing they can do to help heal the world and act as God's partner. The hands should serve as the border for the bulletin board. Over the next few weeks, whenever students do something special to help each other, more fingers can be filled in or more hands can be added.

8. As a follow-up with parents, you may choose to send home another hand and have parents fill in the fingers each time their child helps around the house or helps another person. Or, simply ask them to jot down or share with you things done at home that should be a part of the bulletin board.

Conclusion

1. Take a few minutes to reflect together on the bulletin board. What ideas for helping others did the students write on their fingers? Have them shout out answers.

2. Ask them the following question: Are there more things we can do to help others?

3. Explain that their parents will be on the lookout for ways they are helping at home. Share the homework assignment with them.

4. Have each student complete the sentence: "When I help others I feel good about myself, because…"

SEFER AVODAH: My Jewish Workbook

• Tell students to pay attention to the things they can do now to help other people, that they weren't able to do when they were younger. Explain that they will be filling in the rest of their fingers on the bulletin board by sharing different things they do at school and during the week to help others.

• Explain that at home they will have to complete the following sentences:

I can help others by…

When I help others I feel like God's partner, because…

Date _____

Dear Parents:

This week in class, we learned about how to "hear" God and how to talk to God through prayer and action. Next week we will be talking about how God helps us grow and how, as we grow up, we are better able to take care of ourselves and even help others.

Part of our exploration will focus on how each student is now different from when he or she was a baby. To help facilitate this discussion, please send in a picture of your child as a baby. Make sure that it is a reprint, a spare copy, or an original you don't mind becoming part of an art project that will remain in our school. Together the class will be creating a bulletin board titled "GROWING UP-DOING MY PART." We invite you to come see it and also to take part in it. Return the bottom of this letter with your child's picture and take the time to share with your child some memories of when he or she was little.

At each class for the next several weeks, we will be adding details to this bulletin board of how the students are doing things (in school or at home) to help other people and bring wholeness to our world; this process is called tikkun olam. If your child does something special or particularly kind that you think is worth mentioning on our bulletin board, please drop me a note or stop by to share it.

Thank you for your participation. We look forward to putting together this very special project with you.

Sincerely,

_____

Please fill out and return with the baby picture:

- -

Our child's name is _____

Our favorite thing to watch _____ do when

he/she was a baby was_____

Now that _____ is growing up,

we are proud that he/she has learned to

_____

Photo
Here

Sample Bulletin Board

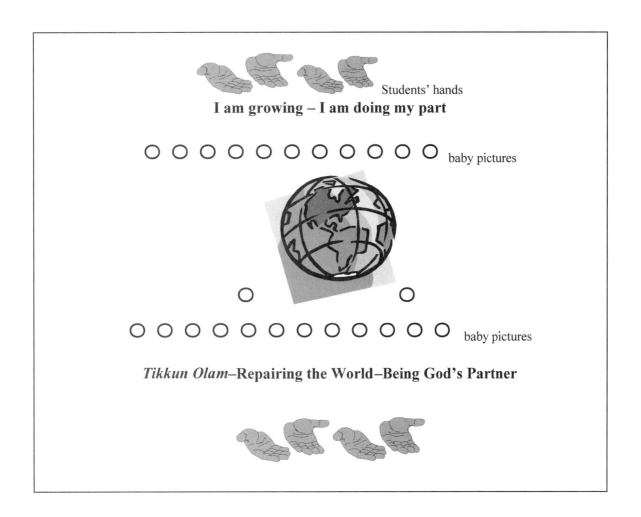

Students' hands

I am growing – I am doing my part

baby pictures

baby pictures

Tikkun Olam–Repairing the World–Being God's Partner

How Does God Talk to Me?

Introduction

The Bible is full of references to moments when God spoke and listened to our Jewish ancestors. "Does God speak to me or hear me?" is a difficult question for young students to grapple with, as it is the concept of the invisibility of God. The foundation of this lesson lays in the idea that we can "hear" God—not with our ears, just as we cannot see God with our eyes (as explained in previous lessons)—when we pay special attention to certain signs of God's "voice" in the world: these "signs" are the feelings we have for things and people around us. These are good feelings that arise when we do the right thing, when we deeply feel within ourselves that something to be glad or proud about has been accomplished: they could be feelings of love, friendship, or happiness, just to mention a few. In this lesson, students will learn to "hear God" by recognizing what causes good feelings and by listening to the voice inside themselves that tells them to do what is right.

Enduring Understanding

➤ *Avodah* is prayer, ceremonies, and celebrations. *Avodah* is the work we do to find sacred connections to God, community, and self.

Essential Questions

1. What can I do to connect to God?

2. What is the evidence that there is a God?

3. How do prayer, ceremonies, and celebrations affect my world?

Questions to be Addressed

1. How can caring for others make us feel good about ourselves?

2. How can identifying feelings help us feel closer to God?

Evidence of Understanding

- Students will design a body picture describing times they used their body to help others and to feel special feelings that helped them feel close to God. For example: I use my hands to comfort my baby brother when he is crying; I can use my eyes to see when someone needs help; I can use my mouth to say prayers for healing or to say nice things to help others feel better; I use my legs and arms to carry food to a food drive for the hungry.

  NOTE: An interesting reading on this subject can be found in *My Body Is Something Special*, by Howard I. Bogot and Daniel B. Syme (New York: UAHC Press, 1998).

Materials Needed

- Markers

- Pencils

- White paper with body outlines on it

- Copies of "The Baby Mouse," by Molly Cone, in *Hello, Hello, Are You There, God?* (New York: UAHC Press, 1999), pp. 9–11

ACTIVITY PLAN

I.　SET INDUCTION: A DISCUSSION OF FEELINGS

1. Ask students to talk about a time when they felt proud for something they did.

2. Ask them to describe what pride feels like.

3. Explain that when we pay attention to our feelings, we can learn important lessons and even feel that God is communicating with us.

Learning Activities

Reading

Read copies of "The Baby Mouse." After reading the story, discuss it by having students answer the following guiding questions:

How does the baby mouse learn about the world around him?

What are the different ways in which the baby mouse learns to "see"?

What, according to the baby mouse's mother, is the most important way to see?

How did the baby mouse show he had learned to "see" with his heart?

How did the baby mouse feel about what he had done to keep the baby bird safe?

Why is the heart the most important way to "see"?

Writing and Art

1. Explain to students that the feeling of pride the mouse felt, and the feelings of pride they described at the opening of the lesson, are one way to hear God "talking" within ourselves. What do they think God is "saying"?

2. Ask students to mention other feelings they think might be messages from God and why. As they make their suggestions, the teacher should write down the list on the board.

3. Tell students that just as the baby mouse was learning about his senses (the teacher should take a moment to review the senses with students) and his body, they can also sometimes "hear" God by paying attention to what their body does.

4. Hand out the "body outlines" (see p. 159). Provide students with pencils and markers. Write on the board:

   What can we do with our bodies to help others?

   What can we do with our bodies to "hear" God talking to us?

5. Lead the class through filling in the body parts. Ask:

   What can we do with our heads …

   What can we do with our eyes? Our mouths? Our ears?…

   What can we do with our hearts?…

   What can we do with our hands? Our feet? …

   … to help others, feel a sense of pride, or get the feeling that God is talking to us?

   Remind students to use the list of feelings brainstormed earlier.

6. As you ask each question, have students fill in their pictures by writing their own answers, or drawing pictures to show an action that answers the question.

III. CONCLUSION

- Have students share their body pictures with the rest of the class.

I "Hear" God ...

Think about the baby mouse in the story we read today and the ways in which the mouse was learning, using all his senses. Think about your body and all that it can do to help others. For each part of your body draw a picture next to it, or write next to it, one thing you can do to help others.

Art by Lisa Rauchwerger

Today I felt good about myself because

_____

_____

_____

_____

_____

When I feel good about myself, I think that God...

_____

_____

_____

_____

_____

Does God Know Me?

Introduction

We have spent eight sessions helping students understand what it means to communicate with God and providing them with tangible skills for doing so. And yet, undoubtedly, many questions remain unanswered. In the previous lesson, we spoke about how God talks to each of us and in this regard the most often-asked question is, "How does God know *me*?" Children wonder how God can recognize each of them individually—how we can feel this unique sense of bond with God and God's presence in our lives?

The creation story teaches us that each of us is created *b'tzelem Elohim* (in God's image). Tradition tells us that we are each created with a unique purpose and that no two people are exactly the same—even if they look very much alike. The struggle is to explain to students how we can be so similar (physically, and sometimes also in our personalities) and yet each be so unique. The story for this lesson reflects that struggle, and it is with this understanding in mind that students can continue to grow toward the Divine and feel free to discover and explore their own unique path to God.

Enduring Understanding

➤ *Avodah* is prayer, ceremonies, and celebrations. *Avodah* is the work we do to find sacred connections to God, community, and self.

Essential Questions

1. How can we find the godliness within ourselves?

2. How can each of us feel our own sense of God's presence?

Evidence of Understanding

- Students will be able to complete their journals by creating a blessing, poem, or picture, which expresses their own personal connection to God.

Materials Needed

- Copies of "The Man Who Was Not Himself," by Molly Cone, in *Hello, Hello, Are You There God?* (New York: UAHC Press, 1999), pp. 15–17

- Mirror

- **The Godliness in Me** worksheet

- Foil

- Blessings worksheet

- Letter for parents

New Vocabulary

b'tzelem Elohim

(*lit.* "in God's image.") A sentence taken from Genesis 1:27, where the story is told of how God created humans in God's image, both male and female. This fundamental idea is at the core of all Jewish values, laying the basis for the belief in the inherent dignity of every human being.

ACTIVITY PLAN

I. SET INDUCTION: STUDENT RECOGNITION GAME

1. Have one student leave the room, explaining that he or she will be called back just in a few minutes to guess "something."

2. The others should select a child to be the "mystery classmate," whom the student waiting outside will have to identify through the various clues the "insiders" will provide.

3. When the excused student returns, he or she will try to identify who the mystery student is—through asking questions about how this mysterious person is dressed, the color of his or her eyes, etc.

4. Play three or four rounds of the game, then discuss:

   • What was it like to be the guesser? What made the game easy? What made it hard?

   • What was it like to be the mystery student?

   • What was it like to be one of the classmates helping the guesser?

   • How do we recognize our friends? (Answer may include the sound of their voice, the clothes they wear, the color of their hair.) Make a list of the answers from this last question on the board.

II. LEARNING ACTIVITIES

Reading

1. Hand out copies of "The Man Who Was Not Himself."

2. After reading the story, ask the following questions:

   • Why did Eli want to look like Mr. Jonathan?

   • What did Eli do to be like Mr. Jonathan?

   • When Eli got sick like Mr. Jonathan and the rabbi came to see him, what did he say to Eli?

   • Why did the rabbi call Eli "Mr. Jonathan"?

   • When Eli was upset because the rabbi called him "Mr. Jonathan," what did the rabbi tell him?

3. Explain that while, like the rabbi in the story said, there is something unique and special about each of us, there is also something about all of us that is the same.

4. Explain that when God created human beings, according to the Torah, God made each of us *b'tzelem Elohim* (in God's image). The teacher should write this sentence on the board, or on a poster using the template from page 170 of this book.

5. Ask students what they think it means to be created "in God's image." Brainstorm ideas and write them on the board or on the poster, under the sentence from Genesis.

I See God in Myself

1. Explain that the class is now going to try to identify what makes us the same and what makes each of us unique.

2. Sit on the floor with the students and pass around a mirror.

3. Ask each student to identify something they see when they look in the mirror that is the same as everyone else (for example, two eyes, a mouth, a nose, and so on).

4. Pass the mirror around once more and ask them to identify one thing they see in the mirror that is unique about them (perhaps the color of their hair or eyes, the way they smile, a beauty mark, freckle, a pair of glasses, etc.).

5. Hand out **The Godliness in Me** worksheet and have students complete it.

III. Conclusion

- The *Avodah* unit is now complete. You can tell students that your hope is that each of them will continue to strive to connect to God, in their own way, a little bit each day.

- Hand out the homework assignment and the letter to parents.

- The last homework assignment should take two weeks to complete. Therefore, be sure to follow up with personal phone calls to make sure that each student completes the assignment.

SEFER AVODAH: My Jewish Workbook

At home

Explain to students that this home assignment will later be posted on a bulletin board. Distribute a worksheet on which students will have to create their own blessing. Allow one to two weeks for students to complete the assignment, giving them time to share their blessings with the class if they so choose.

The Godliness In Me

Glue a round or square piece of foil to the center of this sheet. This page now becomes a mirror. Take a moment to look into your mirror. Reflect on what you see, then fill in the worksheet.

Place your foil mirror here

1. When I look into the mirror, I can see that I am like everyone else because...

_____

_____

_____

2. When I look into the mirror, I can see that I am special because...

_____

_____

_____

3. When I look into the mirror, I know God is in me because...

_____

_____

_____

Date_____

Dear Parents:

Today we completed our unit on Avodah–the prayer, ceremonies, and celebrations we do to find sacred connections to God, community, and self. We have tried to develop an understanding of what it means to communicate with the Divine: through formal prayer, through actions that help others, and through better understanding ourselves. As a culminating activity for the unit, each student was asked to craft his or her own special Avodah. This way, they will create a "tool" to connect with God by remembering all they have learned from this unit and modeling it into a special page of memories, whether in the form of an art project, poem, prayer, or scrapbook-type collage. We have sent home a worksheet to guide them, but we hope that you will work with them as well.

Some wonderful parent resources for talking about God with children are:
- Harold Kushner. When Children Ask about God. New York: Random House, 1995.
- David J. Wolpe. Teaching Your Children About God. New York: HarperCollins, 1995.

We suggest that you have your children explain what they have learned from this study. Your guiding questions may include:

1. The concept of b'tzelem Elohim, being created in God's image (from Genesis 1:27). Ask them to share the worksheet they completed in class today!
2. Why we can't see God, and how we can feel God's help and know God talks to us. (Students learned that God helps us by making us grow, and that God talks to us by helping us feel good about what we can do for others.)
3. Thankfulness. Ask them what they are thankful for, why, and how they express this thankfulness.
4. Ask them what they did during the week that helped them feel good about themselves and helped someone else.

Be sure to share with them some of your feelings and your answers to these questions. Try to complete the worksheet together and have the student return it to class next week. If you have any questions or would like some help with this assignment, please do not hesitate to call.

Looking forward to hearing your child's special blessing,

Sincerely,

_____

My Own Special Way of Connecting With God

Take time to discuss with your parents all you learned about *avodah*—our way to make sacred connections to God. Think about the many things we did in class to connect with God: we wrote blessings of thanks, we thought about what we can do to help others, we learned blessings and prayers, celebrated Shabbat, heard stories and so much more!

Think about how God made you unique, about the ways in which you are a different and special individual. Share your thoughts with your parents. Which ideas and thoughts explored through the study of *avodah* would you like to remember forever? You may want to make a list with your parents, then craft the items on your list into a poem, a scrapbook-type collage, or even a blessing (using the blessing starter words we learned, "Blessed are you, *Adonai* our God, Ruler of the Universe"). No matter what form you decide to give to your collection of thoughts, memories, and ideas from the unit we shared together, this work will become your special *avodah*, your own unique way of connecting with God.

After you have written your blessing, find the proper time to recite it. Then, answer the following questions:

1. What was special about saying this blessing?
2. How did it make me feel to have my own blessing?
3. What does God think of my blessing?

The following sentence can be posted on the blackboard, or pasted in the middle of a large piece of poster board. Ask students what they think this sentence means, and have them write their suggestions on Post-Its that will be glued around the sentence.

b'tzelem Elohim

בְּצֶלֶם אֱלֹהִים

CREATED
IN GOD'S IMAGE

G'milut Chasadim

Melanie Cole Goldberg and Marlene Myerson

Foreword

These nine lessons introduce the second-grade student to the Jewish concept of G'MILUT CHASADIM—personal acts of loving-kindness. At the end of these lessons the students will have gained a basic understanding of what *g'milut chasadim* is, and how they can participate in performing this mitzvah. Students will understand that we learn about *g'milut chasadim* from the Torah and other Jewish sources, that we follow God's example in performing acts of *g'milut chasadim,* and that we can take an active role in performing *g'milut chasadim* in our everyday lives.

All lessons list vocabulary words, materials, and suggested activities. In order to ensure the success of each class, it is important to review the lesson prior to teaching it. Many lessons will need advance preparation, such as finding magazine photographs or bringing in a set of bookends as a prop. Lessons build on one another and are most effective when taught in chronological order.

We wanted to bring your attention to two lessons in particular, numbers seven ("Taking Action") and eight ("Reflections"). These lessons were created to surround an active *g'milut chasadim* experience, either in the community or in the class. "Taking Action" prepares the class for the activity, and "Reflections" serves as a follow-up and review of the activity. We leave the actual activity up to you, as each community has different resources and opportunities. If your activity will take place out in the greater community, you will need to do advance preparation. We wholeheartedly believe in involving the students in the actual **doing** of *g'milut chasadim,* and to this end we included these "action" lessons in our units. These lessons are also an excellent way of involving parents and other adults associated with your class or community. For those schools not equipped to organize this kind of out-of-classroom *g'milut chasadim* experience, alternative suggestions are provided.

We wish you every success with these lessons. We loved creating them and testing them out on second-graders. We hope you will find much joy in teaching them as well.

Making a Difference

Introduction

This lesson introduces the students to the concept of *G'milut Chasadim*—personal acts of lov-ing-kindness. Students are taught that doing *g'milut chasadim* is our duty and that it isn't beyond our reach or too difficult to show personal kindness to others. The lesson starts by showing examples of people helping each other. The story "A Mitzvah is Something Special" provides a good example of how we can be nice to someone even when we feel ambivalent about this other person. By the end of the lesson, the students will be able to share their own examples of doing *g'milut chasadim* through the *G'milut Chasadim Tree* activity. Prior to teaching the lesson, some preparation is needed. The teacher will have to prepare in advance for the "tree" activity and will have to find photos of people helping one another to bring to class. At the end of the lesson, the *G'MILUT CHASADIM DIARY* will be introduced. The purpose of the diary is to connect the work of the class to the students' home life. Each week students should complete a new diary sheet. By the end of the year, the students will have a wonderful collection of examples of things they did to help others.

Enduring Understanding

> ➤ We have a responsibility to perform acts of *g'milut chasadim* to make the world a better, holier place.

Essential Questions

1. Why do we do acts of *g'milut chasadim*?

2. What difference does it make if we do *g'milut chasadim*?

3. How can *g'milut chasadim* make the world a better, holier place?

Evidence of Understanding

- Students will be able to identify examples of an imperfect world and suggest ways in which doing *g'milut chasadim* could make a difference.

- Students will be able to describe how doing *g'milut chasadim* makes a difference in our world.

New Vocabulary

g'milut chasadim	Personal acts of loving-kindness
kadosh	Hebrew word for holy; something sacred, that posseses an element of godliness or has a divine quality
mensch	Yiddish word for a good, decent human being

Material and Resources

- Drawing paper

- Crayons and markers

- Scissors

- Colored construction paper

- Poster board drawn into a tree design or shape (prepare in advance, using brown poster board for a tree trunk and green poster board for leaves)

- Note to parents about the *g'milut chasadim* tree

- Photos (can also be found on various websites), including pictures of people helping others—donating blood, food distribution to the needy, and more. Possible websites to explore to find up-to-date pictures related to contemporary events include: www.redcross.org; www.newyorktimes.com; www.msnbc.com; www.usatoday.com.

The Text

The story "A Mitzvah Is Something Special," by Phyllis Rose Eisenberg.

A Mitzvah Is Something Special by Phyllis Rose Eisenberg

Grandma Esther is my favorite grandma who likes to call me Bubeleh (that means little grandmother) even though my real name is Lisa.

Grandma Esther is my daddy's mother. She says I look just like Daddy did when he was my age, only he was a boy.

Grandma Esther always says, "Take care of your teeth, Bubeleh, so you'll be like me—not a false one in my head and only four fillings."

"Let me see them—let me see them," I say, because she always tells me good stories about her fillings. She opens her mouth wide and there are her four beautiful, solid-gold fillings. "When did you get this one?" I ask, pointing to one in the back.

"When I was going to marry your Grandpa Nathan, I was ashamed that he should have to pay for my dental work. So I saved from my paycheck for a whole year and had this filling done the day before our wedding."

"And what about this one?" I ask, pointing to a bumpy one on top.

"By then," says Grandma Esther, "your daddy was born. But I had no one to leave him with so I could go to the dentist. But when my neighbor, Anna Dubinsky, saw I had a toothache, she said, 'Esther, go. I'll take care of the baby.' So I did. And when I got back, she had already fed and diapered him. Then Bubeleh, she made me hot tea. Oh, it was a real *mitzvah* and I'll never forget it."

"What is a *mitzvah*, Grandma?"

Grandma Esther puts her hands on my shoulders the way she does when she has something important to tell me. "A mitzvah, Lisa, is like a good deed, only much more." Then she looks into my eyes until I feel like some of Grandma Esther is right inside of me. "A mitzvah is a very big blessing. When Anna Dubinsky did what she did, to me *that* was a mitzvah."

Dorrie is my mama's mother. She says I look almost like Mama did when she was a little girl.

Dorrie is my favorite grandma who likes to call me food things like Cookie Pie. And that is really funny because she hardly ever cooks or bakes.

Dorrie wears tinted contacts and has two wigs—a short and a long.

At Dorrie's apartment, I put on her long wig and her green robe and her platform shoes. Then I use my pretend voice and say, "Good morning, I'm your neighbor, Mrs. Noodle Pudding."

"How nice to meet you, Mrs. Pudding," says Dorrie, using her pretend voice, too. "I was just having some gumdrop wine and merry berry pie. Will you join me?"

"No, thank you, Dorrie," I say. "I came here to do you a mitzvah."

"Say, Cookie Pie," says Dorrie, using her own voice, "how do you know about mitzvahs?"

I tell Dorrie about Grandma Esther and Anna Dubinsky. Then I say, "Did you ever have a neighbor like that who did you a mitzvah?"

"Well, Cookie Pie," she says, "when I was little, we knew a flute teacher. He was very poor so my mother and father gave him food and clothes. He wanted to do something nice, too, so he gave me free flute lessons."

"Were the lessons fun?"

"No, I had to practice every day for two whole years. Oh, how I hated it!"

"But Dorrie, how could that be a mitzvah?"

"I didn't know it was a mitzvah then, Lisa, but I know it now. Now I love to play the flute."

"But are mitzvahs only for grown-ups?"

"I don't know, Cookie Pie," says Dorrie, "I never thought about it."

"Dorrie, would you pour some gumdrop wine while I think about it?"

While I sip my wine and eat my merry berry pie, I keep wondering if I will know when a mitzvah happens to me. I hope I do.

Grandma Esther is a very good cook and baker and she is teaching me how to make strudel. So far I'm adding the nuts and raisins and preheating the oven to 350°. Someday she's going to let me roll the dough all by myself. When I learn how to make strudel all the way, I might teach Dorrie how to do it.

Grandma Esther is also very good at making quilts. Whenever I sleep over, I sleep in her bed and she always tucks me in with a beautiful quilt she made long ago.

"A bubeleh like you should go to sleep early," Grandma Esther always says, even though I tell her that at home I watch TV until I fall asleep. (It only happened once, but I keep forgetting to tell her that part.) "You've got to grow," she says.

"I'm always growing," I say. "Even when my eyes are open."

"I don't like you to be up so late. Good night, my Bubeleh," she says, and we give each other some big, squishy hugs.

Later, I turn on the light and count the quilt squares. So far I'm up to eight daisies, fourteen polka dots, nine roses and twelve stripes. If I ever take quilt lessons, I'll make one with a million squares so it will be big enough for Grandma and me when we're older and bigger.

Dorrie has a very long hair growing out of her chin that you can see only in bright light. When I say, "Dorrie, your chin hair grew again," she stops what she's doing and pulls it out. Then she says, "What would I do without you, Cookie Pie?"

Dorrie has lots of pictures on her walls and so many plants I think I'm in a pretty forest. Gus painted all the pictures and he grows the plants, too. Gus is Dorrie's friend.

At Dorrie's, I sleep on her living-room sofa, except when her friend Sandra is there. Then Dorrie calls me and says, "Sandra's sleeping over this weekend, Lisa. You'll have to come another time."

"How come, Dorrie?" I say. "How come Sandra gets to sleep over and not me?"

"She's very lonely, Cookie Pie. Her best friend moved away. So I'll try to cheer her up."

"When Sandra stays with you, are you doing a mitzvah?"

"I don't know, Cookie Pie," Dorrie says, "I just know that people are happier when they're not lonely. . . . Lisa, how about coming here next weekend—okay?"

"It's not so okay, Dorrie," I say. "I was planning to visit you this weekend. Why can't someone else cheer up Sandra?"

"Sandra needs me," says Dorrie. And then her voice gets wrinkly and she says, "I'm sorry to disappoint you, Cookie Pie. I really am."

When she says it like that, I know she understands my sadness. So I say, "Okay, Dorrie, see you next weekend." But I'm still not very happy.

I wonder if Sandra thinks it's a mitzvah that Dorrie is going to cheer her up? I would, because Dorrie is very good at cheering.

I hope that a mitzvah happens to me before I am very much older.

When I tell Grandma Esther about Dorrie's cheering Sandra, she says, "That reminds me of Grandpa Nathan. He cheered people, too." Then Grandma Esther nods the way she does when she thinks of Grandpa Nathan.

"What was he like?" I ask. She has already told me, but I like to hear it again.

"He was as good as gold. There wasn't a mean streak in his whole body. If only he could have lived to see my little Bubeleh," says Grandma Esther. "Lisa, do you know what I pray every night—every night so help me?"

"What, Grandma?"

"That I live long enough to dance at your wedding. And that you will have a good man like Nathan so you can have a good life."

"My daddy says that a good life means doing whatever means a lot to you. And that I should be thinking about that right now."

And Grandma Esther smiles and says, "Your daddy is a smart man and a good man. He's just like your Grandpa Nathan."

I tell Dorrie about my Grandpa Nathan, and she says, "Your Grandpa Al is just the opposite. He's loaded with mean streaks. It was good riddance when he left."

"Where did he go, Dorrie?"

"Who knows? Maybe he's on a mountaintop somewhere, or living in a lemon tree or—"

"No one could live in a lemon tree," I say.

Dorrie puckers up her mouth until her crease disappears. "Grandpa Al is a lemon, Cookie Pie, so he'd be right at home." And she laughs so hard I think she will never stop. Finally she says, "Believe me, Lisa, I don't miss him."

"Would you miss Gus?"

"Yes," she says. "I like Gus."

I like Gus, too. Especially when he makes hot dogs on a hibachi out on Dorrie's balcony. And plays his guitar while Dorrie plays her flute. Gus sings songs that sometimes make me sad, but I like then anyhow. I even know the words to three of them.

I tell Dorrie, "I might be a folk singer when I grow up, or maybe an actress."

"Whatever you do," she says, "you'll always be my Cookie Pie."

"But, Dorrie, what if I grow up and become president of everything—you couldn't call me Cookie Pie then!"

"I'd call you President Cookie Pie."

"Would you bake strudel for me if I was president?"

"No, Lisa, I wouldn't."

"But, Dorrie, wouldn't you be proud of me if I was president of everything in the world."

"I'll always be proud of you, Cookie Pie, but I'll never bake strudel. Period."

I guess that Dorrie will never do things she doesn't care about. But for things she likes, like gumdrop wine and music and cheering, there's no one like Dorrie.

And there's no one like Grandma Esther for strudel and quilts and weddings, because that is what she's good at.

For stories, Dorrie is the best in the world for the mean-streak kind. But for the gold-filling kind and the good-as-gold kind, no one is better than Grandma Esther.

I thought Dorrie and Grandma Esther cared about everything different, but they both care about me. So one might when my parents were going out . . . I invited them to sleep over.

Esther, your strudel is delicious," says Dorrie. "And your music makes me dance," says Grandma Esther.

"This seems like a mitzvah," I say. "Is it?" "It's such a big mitzvah, Lisa," Grandma Esther says . . ." That we'll remember it forever," says Dorrie.

From *A Mitzvah Is Something Special* by Phyllis Rose Eisenberg, illustrated by Susan Jeschke. New York: Harper and Row, Publishers, 1978. Used with permission of the publisher.

ACTIVITY PLAN

I.   SET INDUCTION

Show students up to six different images of people helping others. Ask them what they think is happening in the photos. Ask them to try to imagine what the people in the pictures may be feeling.

II.   LEARNING ACTIVITIES

Listing Activity

1. Make two columns on the board: (1) Difficult situations shown in the pictures; (2) How are people trying to help?

2. Reflecting on the pictures shown in the Set Induction, have students respond to each heading. The teacher will fill in the columns as students give their answers.

3. Continue by soliciting other examples from the students for both columns. (The teacher may encourage them to think of things close to home, too.)

Example:

DIFFICULT SITUATION	HOW ARE PEOPLE HELPING?
Homeless people sitting on sidewalk	Volunteers handing out sleeping bags

Questions for Discussion

Helping others with our kind, loving actions is what we call *g'milut chasadim*. Doing *g'milut chasadim* is considered holy (*kadosh*) because by performing acts of loving-kindness we help God make the world a better place. Things or actions that connect us to God are *kadosh*.

1. How were all the examples we listed on the board acts of *g'milut chasadim*?

2. What makes those acts of *g'milut chasadim* special, sacred, *kadosh*?

3. Ask the students to think about what they do in their lives that could be considered acts of *g'milut chasadim*—acts of loving-kindness.

4. What are other things that they can do both physically (with their hands and work) and spiritually (with their hearts) to help fix our imperfect world? (Examples could include anything that the student does personally to assist someone else, such as caring for a sick person, feeding the family pet, welcoming a new classmate.)

Story Activity

1. Ask students to define the word "mensch." Ask them to give examples of people who are menschs and ask them to explain why. Then ask them what they think the connection is between a mensch and doing *g'milut chasadim*.

2. Read the story *A Mitzvah Is Something Special.* Stress the importance of listening carefully to this reading. Afterward, ask the following questions:

   • What did Lisa learn about her Grandpa Nathan from her grandma?

   • What things did her grandpa do that demonstrated that he was a mensch?

   • What is a "mensch"?

   • How were these acts of *g'milut chasadim*?

   • How does the grandma show that she is a mensch?

- What does Lisa do at the end of the story that shows that she is also a mensch?

- How does this story show that acts of *g'milut chasadim* can be part of our everyday lives?

Art Activity

1. Have students draw a picture of themselves doing an act of *g'milut chasadim*, a personal act that involves helping or being there for others.

2. Have students put a title on their drawing. The drawings can be used for a bulletin board display, or students can take their drawing home to share with their families.

III. CONCLUSION

- Show students the *G'milut Chasadim* Tree that the teacher has created in advance on the bulletin board. Explain that they can help this tree grow fruit by doing acts of *g'milut chasadim*. Provide students with fruit shapes they can trace and cut out on colored construction paper. The students should complete the following sentence on their piece of fruit:

    My Act of *G'milut Chasadim* Was _____.

- Add the fruit to the tree.

- Ask students: What difference does it make if we do *g'milut chasadim*?

- How did your act of *g'milut chasadim* make the world a better and holier place?

    NOTE: The teacher should prepare a note to parents asking them to encourage their child(ren) to do acts of *g'milut chasadim*. A few minutes should be set aside each week for the students to add additional *g'milut chasadim* fruits to the tree.

Opportunities to Do G'milut Chasadim

Introduction

This lesson breaks the broad concept of *g'milut chasadim* into smaller components. As they go from station to station and figure out the riddles, students will learn that there are specific Jewish acts within the larger *g'milut chasadim* category, and that each act of *g'milut chasadim* has a specific Hebrew name: for example, "visiting the sick" corresponds to the Jewish value of "*bikur cholim.*" It is important to set up the stations before the students enter class. Not only will the lesson be prepared but the students may see the stations and be curious about what they will be learning that day.

Enduring Understanding

➤ We have a responsibility to perform acts of *g'milut chasadim* to make the world a better, holier place.

Essential Questions

1. Why do we do acts of *g'milut chasadim*?

2. What difference does it make if we do *g'milut chasadim*?

Evidence of Understanding

• Identify opportunities to do acts of *g'milut chasadim*

• Experience an act of *g'milut chasadim*, reflect on it, and analyze its impact on both the doer and the receiver

New Vocabulary

kadosh   Hebrew word for holy; something sacred, that posseses an ele-
                            ment of godliness, or has a divine quality.

Talmud   The comprehensive body of Jewish traditions and laws, com-
                            prised of the Mishnah and Gemara, written in the rabbinic peri-
                            od (165 B.C.E.-600 C.E.).

                            [For the students] A book of Jewish laws and stories written by
                            the ancient Rabbis. The Talmud is still used today as a source of
                            learning and a guide for Jewish living.

Materials and Resources

- Pictures with riddles written underneath (see pp. 191–198)

- Colored construction paper

- Markers and/or crayons

- Bookends

- Letter to Parents

- Diary Sheet

The Text

"Rabbi Simlai taught: The Torah begins with deeds of loving-kindness and ends with
deeds of loving-kindness. It begins with deeds of loving-kindness, as it is written, 'And
God made for Adam and for his wife garments of skins and clothed them' (Genesis
3:21). It ends with deeds of loving-kindness, as it is written, 'And God buried him
(Moses) in the valley in the land of Moab' (Deuteronomy 34:6)."

Sotah 14a

ACTIVITY PLAN

I. SET INDUCTION

Ask students to explain what a riddle is (i.e., a tricky question; a question with clues that help
you find the answer). Sometimes riddles are funny and sometimes they're not, but they are

always a little tricky. Give students examples (e.g., "What is black and white and red (read) all over?"-A newspaper). Ask them to give examples of riddles.

II. Learning Activities

Solving Riddles

1. Show the students a pair of bookends. Ask the following riddle: How is the Torah like a pair of bookends? Brainstorm some possible answers. Tell them that they can find clues to the answer in the quote from the Jewish text.

2. Hand out copies of the text from page 199. Read the text out loud to the class.

3. Explain to the students that to understand this riddle we need to know that the Torah has five books (or sections). Write the names of the books in order so that Genesis and Deuteronomy are bracketing the other names. You may want to write these names in a different color or in a different design—something to make them stand out. For example:

Genesis, Exodus, Leviticus, Numbers, Deuteronomy

Show how the quote about God making garments for Adam and Eve is from the first book, the Book of Genesis, and the quote about God burying Moses is in the last one, Deuteronomy. The Torah teaches from the beginning to the end about *g'milut chasadim*. The riddle makes sense in a visual way. It looks like Genesis and Deuteronomy are bookends to the other books in the Torah. Ask the students to solve some other *g'milut chasadim* riddles (see "What can you do to help?" pp. 191–198). Hang five pictures with riddles around the classroom (see "*G'milut Chasadim* Riddles" below). Give students an answer sheet, numbered 1-5, on which to record their answers. In groups (or pairs), the students will move from picture to picture, reading the clues and answering the question: What would you need or wish for, if you were the person in the picture? What can you do to help?

G'milut Chasadim Riddles
(Choose five)

Visiting the Sick   *Bikur Cholim*

My nose is all drippy, there's pounding in my head.

What can you do if your friend's stuck in bed?

Welcoming Guests/Strangers   *Hachnasat Orchim*

I'm new at your school. I have just moved here.

What can you do to bring me some cheer?

Helping People   *V'ahavta L'rei-acha Kamocha*

I live next door and I just had a baby.

What can you do to help a tired lady?

Caring for Animals   *Tzaar Baalei Chayyim*

I'm just a puppy, can't do much on my own.

What can you do besides giving me a bone?

Honoring (Visiting) the Elderly   *Kibud Z'keinim*

I'm old and gray, and life for me can be a bore.

What can you do to make my spirits soar?

Feeding the Hungry   *Maachil R'eivim*

My stomach is grumbling, there's no food for us to eat.

What can you do to help 'til we get on our feet?

Comforting Someone Who Is Sad   *Nechamah*

My eyes can't stop crying, I'm feeling so sad.

What can you do to make me feel glad?

Clothing the Naked   *Malbish Arumim*

My clothes are all tattered; we're very poor, you see.

What can you do to be kind to me?

Conclusion

- Discuss answers as a class. Ask students to share personal experiences related to each picture (situation).

- Make a list of the various opportunities to do *g'milut chasadim* that the students learned from the riddles.

Sample answer sheet

Riddle 1

What would you need or wish for, if you were the person in the picture?

_____

What can you do to help?_____

Riddle 2

What would you need or wish for if you were the person in the picture?_____

What can you do to help?_____

Riddle 3

What would you need or wish for if you were the person in the picture?_____

What can you do to help?_____

Riddle 4

What would you need or wish for if you were the person in the picture?_____

What can you do to help?_____

Riddle 5

What would you need or wish for if you were the person in the picture?_____

What can you do to help?_____

Role Playing (Optional)

- Have students choose one of the above situations to role-play.

- Encourage those students who are watching to give alternative interpretations by calling out "Freeze!" and replacing one of the actors.

III. CONCLUSION

There are many different ways to do *g'milut chasadim*. Have students look at the list and share ideas of opportunities they may have for *g'milut chasadim* at home or in their community.

1. Ask each student to choose one act of *g'milut chasadim* from the list that he or she would like to do in the coming week, and record the performance of this act in his or her *G'MILUT CHASADIM* Diary.

G'MILUT CHASADIM DIARY

Explain to the students that a diary is a book in which we write down the things we do and emotions we feel. Give each student a letter for the parents, in which the teacher explains what the *G'milut Chasadim* Diary is. A diary sheet is to be completed each week after performing an act of *g'milut chasadim*.

Date_____

Dear Parents:

We hope that your child(ren) will share some of what we are doing in religious school.

In our class, students will be studying the importance in our Jewish tradition and daily lives of g'milut chasadim-personal acts of loving-kindness. They will be examining stories from the Torah in which g'milut chasadim takes place, and they will be able to connect the ancient texts of our people to our own contemporary lives.

Your child's homework will be done each week on the pages of the G'MILUT CHASADIM DIARY. The purpose of this diary is to help each student record the performance of conscious acts of g'milut chasadim. The personal nature of these acts of loving-kindness is perhaps the most important aspect of the exercises to be stressed (examples of personal g'milut chasadim may include: helping a parent or sibling with a project or task; taking care of a pet; hosting a guest; caring for someone who is ill by making a card or picture and sending it to the person; comforting someone who is sad, and so on).

One of the enduring understandings of g'milut chasadim is the relationship we have to God. When we do an act of g'milut chasadim, we are acting like God wants us to act. And, by performing personal acts of loving-kindness, we are engaging in holy work. One of the questions in the diary will ask the students what they think is holy (kadosh) about that particular act of g'milut chasadim they have performed. This may be explained by asking what felt special about doing it, or how this act is comparable to the work of God. The idea is that even something as common as feeding a pet is essentially holy. Taking a personal responsibility and acting in a kind way makes our world a better place and enables us to help bring more holiness into the world.

I encourage you to discuss these ideas with your child, as each week she/he will be asked to work at home on a different sheet of the G'MILUT CHASADIM Diary.

Thank you for your support and participation in your child's Jewish learning. If you have any questions about this or any other aspect of our class, please feel free to contact me through the religious school.

Sincerely,

_____

G'MILUT CHASADIM diary

name:_____date:_____

The act of *g'milut chasadim* that I did:

Where I did it:_____

_____

When I did it:_____

_____

For whom I did it:_____

_____

With whom I did it:_____

_____

How it made me feel:_____

_____

What I learned by doing it:_____

_____

What was *kadosh* (holy) about this act
of loving-kindness:_____

_____

On the other side, draw a picture or attach a photo of
yourself doing your act of *g'milut chasadim.*

What can you do to help?

My nose is all drippy, there's pounding in my head.

What can you do if your friend's stuck in bed?

Bikur Cholim

What can you do to help?

I'm new at your school, I have just moved here.

What can you do to bring me some cheer?

Hachnasat Orchim

What can you do to help?

I live next door and I just had a baby.

What can you do to help a tired lady?

V'ahavta L'rei-acha Kamocha

What can you do to help?

I'm just a puppy, can't do much on my own.

What can you do besides giving me a bone?

Tzaar Baalei Chayim

What can you do to help?

I'm old and gray, and life for me can be a bore.

What can you do to make my spirits soar?

Kibud Z'keinim

What can you do to help?

My stomach is grumbling, there's no food for us to eat.

What can you do to help 'til we get on our feet?

Maachil R'eivim

What can you do to help?

My eyes can't stop crying, I'm feeling so sad.

What can you do to make me feel glad?

Nechamah

What can you do to help?

My clothes are all tattered; we're very poor, you see.

What can you do to be kind to me?

Malbish Arumim

Reading From the Talmud

"Rabbi Simlai taught: The Torah begins with deeds of loving-kindness and ends with deeds of loving-kindness. It begins with deeds of loving-kindness, as it is written, 'And God made for Adam and for his wife garments of skins and clothed them' (Genesis 3:21). It ends with deeds of loving-kindness, as it is written, 'And God buried him (Moses) in the valley in the land of Moab' (Deuteronomy 34:6)."

Sotah 14

Torah Teaches Us

Introduction

The most important aspect of this lesson is to connect acts of *g'milut chasadim* to the Torah. The goal is for students to learn that the Torah is a source of moral and ethical teaching for life. The biblical stories of our ancestors contained in the Torah set an example and teach us that, as Jews, we have an obligation to do good things and to be good people. Furthermore, this lesson asks students to personalize the teachings from the Torah by picturing themselves acting as one of the positive Jewish biblical characters.

Enduring Understanding

➤ We have a responsibility to perform acts of *g'milut chasadim* to make the world a better, holier place.

Essential Questions

1. Why do we do acts of *g'milut chasadim*?

2. How does doing *g'milut chasadim* connect us to God?

3. How can we learn about *g'milut chasadim* from the Torah?

Evidence of Understanding

- Students will be able to identify acts of *g'milut chasadim* found in stories from the Torah and other Jewish sources.

- Students will act out stories from the Torah and analyze and express their roles in doing *g'milut chasadim* through drawing, speaking, writing, and role-playing.

- The class will reflect on how we are like God when we do personal acts of *g'milut chasadim*.

- Students will analyze their acts of *g'milut chasadim* and compare them to God's actions as illustrated by stories from Jewish tradition.

Material and Resources

- Torah stories written on poster board (see page 203)

- Markers, crayons, and construction paper

- Worksheet

The Text

Ben Bag Bag said, "Read the Torah over and over and over again. There is always something new that you can learn from it."

Pirkei Avot 5:25

ACTIVITY PLAN

I. SET INDUCTION

- Ask the students to share one new thing that they learned this week. (Example: a new fact, a new Hebrew word, or a new skill.) Ask them to share one new thing they learned about something they *already* knew. (Example: additional information about a familiar subject or a new way of doing something.) Ask them if they relearned something they already knew. Ask how they learn new things. (Answers may include: from teachers, parents, books, television, and each other.)

- Read together with the class the sentence from *Pirkei Avot* 5:25. Explain that the sentence was written a long time ago by a rabbi with a very unusual name—Rabbi Ben Bag Bag—who thought that the Torah could be a great teacher.

- Ask students: How do you think the Torah can be a teacher?

II. Learning Activities

Stories from the Torah

1. Set up five stations, each with a narration from Torah (see p. 203) written on poster board or chart paper.

2. Divide the class into groups of three.

3. Ask each group to read the short Torah story and decide what act of *g'milut chasadim* God performed in the story.

   NOTE: The list of acts of *g'milut chasadim* (see p. 204) can be posted beneath each story.

4. When the groups have completed the assignment, bring the class together and have them report on their choices.

5. Write the appropriate act of *g'milut chasadim* beneath each of the five Torah stories.

The Torah Stations
Five Brief Biblical Narrations

Station I

1. God created Adam and Eve, the first man and woman. They lived in the Garden of Eden. And God made for Adam and his wife Eve garments of skins and clothed them. (Genesis 2:7-Genesis 3:21)

Station II

2. Abraham sent his servant, Eliezer, to find a wife for Isaac. When Eliezer arrived at the well, God sent Rebekah to offer water for his camels so that Eliezer would know what a kind person she was. (Genesis 24:1-27)

Station III

3. When Abraham was not feeling well, God sent angels to visit him. (Genesis 18:1-15)

Station IV

4. Isaac was the son of Abraham and Sarah. When Isaac's mother died, Isaac was very sad and God comforted him by providing a wife to love him. (Genesis 24:63-67)

Station V

5. When Moses led the Israelites out of Egypt, they traveled through the desert for many days and many nights. When they had no food and felt very hungry, God provided manna for them to eat. (Exodus 16:1-8)

Note: Copy each of these narrations on to a large sheet of poster board or chart paper, one on each sheet.

Acts of *G'milut Chasadim*

נֶחָמָה

Comforting the mourner   *Nechamah*

מַלְבִּישׁ עֲרֻמִּים

Clothing the naked   *Malbish arumim*

בִּקּוּר חוֹלִים

Visiting the sick   *Bikur cholim*

מַאֲכִיל רְעֵבִים

Feeding the hungry   *Maachil r'eivim*

הַכְנָסַת אוֹרְחִים

Welcoming guests/strangers   *Hachnasat orchim*

וְאָהַבְתָּ לְרֵעֲךָ כָּמוֹךָ

Treating people with kindness   *V'ahavta l'rei-acha kamocha*

צַעַר בַּעֲלֵי חַיִּים

Being kind to animals   *Tzaar baalei chayim*

כִּבּוּד זְקֵנִים

Honoring the Elderly   *Kibud Z'keinim*

Note: Copy this sheet and place beneath each biblical narration

G'milut Chasadim **Skit**

- Working in groups, have students choose one of the ideas from the Torah stories and create an original skit based on an act of *g'milut chasadim*—like the ones God did in the story.

- Each group will then perform it in front of the class, while the other students must identify the act of *g'milut chasadim* "staged" by their classmates.

Personalizing *G'milut Chasadim*

- Review the Torah stories about *g'milut chasadim*.

- Ask the students to choose the story they liked the most and answer the following questions (see worksheet, p. 206):

    1. I picked this Torah story because_____

    2. The act of *g'milut chasadim* that I learned from this Torah story is
    _____

    3. I could do this act of *g'milut chasadim* by _____

    4. I think that doing this act of *g'milut chasadim* will help me be like God because
    _____

- Have students draw a picture of themselves doing this act of *g'milut chasadim*.

III.   CONCLUSION

- Ask the students to sit in a circle on the floor.

- Read Ben Bag Bag's statement again. Ask each student to share one new thing that the Torah taught him or her today.

- Write their answers on strips of colored construction paper: "The Torah taught me_____."

- Create a bulletin board display titled "The Torah is Our Teacher!" containing the students' answers, pictures from the "Personalizing *G'milut Chasadim*" activity, and their concluding comments written on strips of colored construction paper.

Personalizing *G'milut Chasadim*

The Torah story I chose is_____

_____

I picked this Torah story because_____

_____

The act of *g'milut chasadim* that I learned from this Torah story is_____

_____

I could do this act of *g'milut chasadim* by_____

_____

I think that doing this act of *g'milut chasadim* will help me be like God because_____

_____

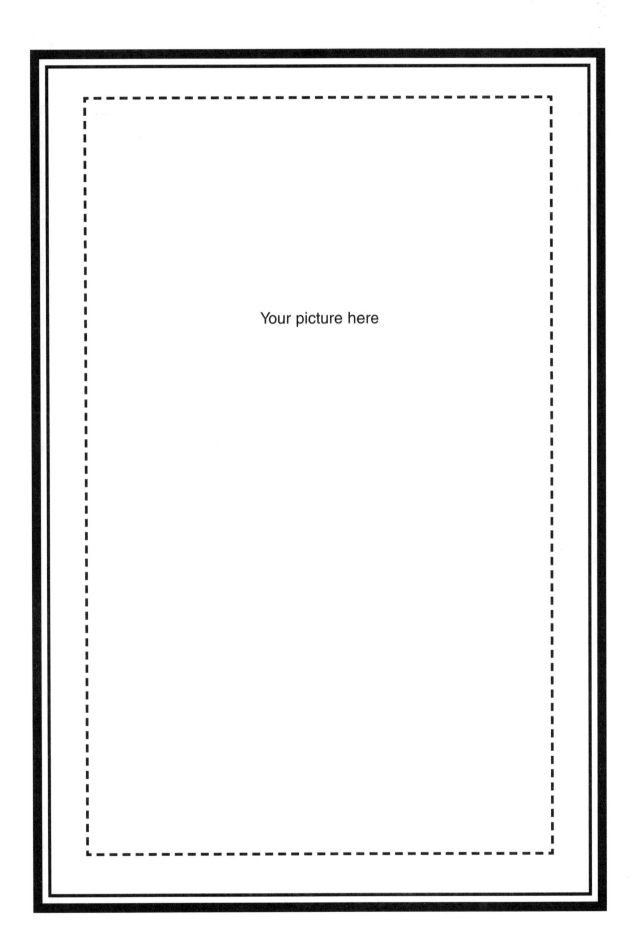
Your picture here

In God's Image

Introduction

This lesson introduces the concept of *b'tzelem Elohim*. Torah teaches us that every human being is created in God's image (*b'tzelem Elohim*), and that we have the ability to act as God wants us to. Because we are created in God's image, we can be partners with God by caring for and helping others every day. By choosing to do *g'milut chasadim,* we choose to be like God. In order for this lesson to be successful, all the "Mystery Hunt" materials must be prepared and set up prior to class. A hot-glue gun is recommended in the creation of your "*B'tzelem Elohim* Mirrors." However, all precautions must be taken in using this potentially dangerous item, which should be handled exclusively by an adult.

Enduring Understanding

➤ We have a responsibility to perform acts of *g'milut chasadim* to make the world a better, holier place.

Essential Questions

1. Why do we do acts of *g'milut chasadim*?

2. How does doing acts of *g'milut chasadim* connect us to God?

3. How can we learn about *g'milut chasadim* from the Torah?

Evidence of Understanding

• Students reflect on how we are like God when we do acts of *g'milut chasadim* for other people.

Background for Teacher

God and Anthropomorphism

"God is not a person or a thing. No one can draw a picture or make a statue of God. God cannot be adequately described in words. But sometimes, in order to share information about God in a way that others can understand, we use human images to describe God. The process of using human characteristics, language, and images to describe something nonhuman is called anthropomorphism. The Bible often uses anthropomorphisms such as 'God made,' 'God saw,' and 'God rested' to help the reader understand God's actions. Sometimes the Bible ascribes human body parts to God so that the reader has a better frame of reference from which to understand God's actions. Although we know that God has no body and does not have a mouth, hands, or eyes, anthropomorphisms help give us an immediate (albeit simplistic) understanding of God."

Steven Steinbock, *A Teacher's Guide to Torah:*
The Growing Gift (New York: UAHC Press, 1994), pp. 10-11.

New Vocabulary

b'tzelem Elohim   *lit.* "[Created] in the image of God"

Bibliography

Steinbock, Steven. *Torah: The Growing Gift.* New York: UAHC Press, 1994.

Material and Resources

- Small mirrors and copies of the text from Genesis 1:27, each gift-wrapped in a box and placed in different locations

- Copies of the text from Genesis 1:27 written on small cards

- "Mystery Hunt" clues

- Pictures of people doing things for one another (these can be taken from magazines, or drawn by the students)

- Colored sticky dots

- Quick-dry clay

• Pieces of reflective materials

• Assorted glass beads, ribbons, etc.

The Text

"And God created man and woman in God's image."

Genesis 1:27

ACTIVITY PLAN

I.   SET INDUCTION

1. Ask students if they have ever wondered what God looks like. Encourage them to share their ideas.

2. Explain that no one knows for sure what God looks like, but today they are going to search for clues that will help them discover God's "reflection."

II.   LEARNING ACTIVITIES

Mystery Hunt

1. Divide the class into groups of two or three. Give each group a clue about where to search for the "mysterious objects."

   Examples:

   • Look for something small and special in the sanctuary.

   • Look for something small and special under the teacher's desk.

   • Look for something small and special on the desk in the school office.

2. Each group will find a box containing a small gift-wrapped mirror, along with the text, "And God created man and woman in God's image."

3. Bring students back together in a circle to unwrap the boxes and talk about what they contain. Ask:

   • What do we see when we look in the mirror?

- Read the text "And God created man and woman in God's image." What do you think this sentence means?

- The Jewish people believe that God is invisible. But if God is invisible, what does the Torah mean when it says that God made man and woman "in God's image"?

- If we all look different, how could we all still be created in God's image?

4. Introduce the phrase *"b'tzelem Elohim"* (in the image of God). Stress God-like behaviors, as opposed to physical attributes. Some people think God "appears" through acts of loving-kindness (*g'milut chasadim*):

  - How can each of us be like God?

  - How can each of us behave like God?

Looking for God

Have pictures of people doing things for one another spread out on the tables. Ask the students to find the places in the pictures where people are doing the kinds of things God would want them to do and place colored sticky dots on those places. Encourage them to help each other. Bring the students back together to talk about where they placed dots and why they chose to put the dots there.

Wall Decoration

Create a wall decoration using quick-dry clay, pieces of reflective material, glass beads, ribbons, etc. that can hang on each student's bedroom wall to serve as a reminder that he or she is created in the image of God.

III. CONCLUSION

Have the students gather in circle. Have each student look into his or her wall decoration and complete the sentence: "I am like God when I..."

Being God's Partner

Introduction

This lesson moves deeper into the exploration of how we can be God's partners through our acts of loving-kindness. Its central activity is a guided visualization, which should be conducted in a quiet and calm environment for it to be most effective. A fun exercise for this lesson is the poster activity. The three *g'milut chasadim* posters of paper hands and hearts that students create will make a beautiful bulletin board display for the classroom or the school hallway. Depending on your time, you may want the children themselves to trace and cut out their paper hands and hearts for the poster activity.

Enduring Understanding

➤ We have a responsibility to perform acts of *g'milut chasadim* to make the world a better, holier place.

Essential Questions

1. Why do we do acts of *g'milut chasadim*?

2. How does doing *g'milut chasadim* connect us to God?

3. How can *g'milut chasadim* make the world a better, holier place?

Evidence of Understanding

• Students will reflect on how their acts of *g'milut chasadim* make them God's partner.

Materials and Resources

- Colored construction paper hands and hearts

- Glue sticks

- Markers

- Three large sheets of poster board

The Text

Syme, Deborah Shayne. *Partners*. New York: UAHC Press, 1990.

(Alternative selection: Sasso, Sandy Eisenberg, *God's Paintbrush*. Woodstock, Vermont: Jewish Lights, 1992.)

ACTIVITY PLAN

I. SET INDUCTION

Ask the class to talk about what it means when you are someone's partner.

II. LEARNING ACTIVITIES

Story

Read "Partners" by Deborah Shayne Syme and ask the following questions:

- What do we see around us that lets us know that the world needs our help?

- How could the children in the story show us that they were helping God?

- How can we help God?

- What would we need to do and how would we need to act to show God that we are partners in making the world a better place?

- How does performing acts of *g'milut chasadim* make us partners with God?

Guided Visualization Exercise

Background Information

Guided visualization is a technique used to help people experience their feelings and thoughts in a relaxed and controlled setting. Participants are encouraged to close their eyes and relax while the leader (teacher) slowly and carefully uses words, in a gentle soothing way, to bring participants on an imaginary journey of self-exploration. The visualization leader sets a scene, describes events, and guides participants through these mental settings.

Visualization

Ask the students to sit comfortably, to find a place or position where they can feel totally at ease. Ask them to close their eyes and listen as the teacher takes them on a guided visualization to explore ways in which they act as God's partners at home, at school, and in their community. (For suggestions on how to guide the visualization, see pp. 215–216.)

G'milut Chasadim Link Activity

1. Set up three stations around the classroom.

2. Post a large sheet of poster board at each station with one of the following titles:

   1. Home   2. School   3. Community

3. At each station, place cutouts of colored hands and hearts, markers, and glue sticks.

4. Instruct students to move from station to station, choose a hand or heart and write on it the answer to the following statements:

   I am God's partner at home when I:_____

   I am God's partner at school when I:_____

   I am God's partner in my neighborhood when I:_____

5. Have the students glue their completed hands and hearts to the posters.

   Gather the students in a large group. Talk about some of their answers and why they chose those particular examples.

III. CONCLUSION

- In a circle, do a reflection whip by passing around a sign that says: "Ask me how I am God's partner."

- After answering the question, each student will pass the sign to another classmate.

Guided Visualization

(Read very slowly in a soft, soothing voice. Pause between sentences.)

We are going to take a journey on the wings of our imaginations. Now I would like you to find a comfortable place to sit or lie down. If you like, you may close your eyes as you listen to my voice. I will guide you with my voice as you use your imagination. During this imaginary journey, don't talk—just listen and think. I may be asking you questions, but don't answer me aloud. Just think the answers in your mind. Take a slow deep breath and feel your lungs fill up with air. Now quietly let the breath go out and feel your body relax. Once more, take a deep breath in… and let it out. Take a deep breath… let it out. Each time you take the air in, you feel your body and your mind getting relaxed. Let all your thoughts disappear and just listen to my voice as I guide you.

Imagine that you are in your bedroom at home. Use your imagination to look around and see your room. Look at your bed, your closet, and your walls. Look everywhere. See in your mind everything that is there. Now walk outside of your bedroom and go through your house. Walk slowly through all the rooms. Think about what you see. Think about your family. What other family members can you see at home as you slowly walk through the house? As you think about your house and your family, imagine that you see something on your kitchen table that is broken. Picture in your mind this broken object. Who or what do you see? What can you do to help? Imagine that you are acting like God's partner as you are helping. How do you feel when you are helping? How can you tell that what you did was good? You did a good job. You were being God's partner, doing *g'milut chasadim*.

Listen to my voice as I bring you to another place. This time we are not going to be in your house, but we are going to be in your school. Imagine that you are in your classroom. It can be in this same class or in your regular class during the week. Imagine that you are in the classroom and see all the things that are there. In your mind, see your teachers, your classmates, the decorations on the walls and the desks or tables. Everything is going well. You are having a great day. You are learning something that makes you feel good. As you imagine your class, something catches your eye. You see that your friend has a sad expression. Think about how you can help. How do you make the situation better? What happens when you start to help? Do things get better? How do you feel about helping your friend? How did you just act like God's partner?

Let's continue on our imaginary journey. Use your imagination so that you find yourself in your neighborhood. Your neighborhood is special to you because it is where you live. You have houses and shops in your neighborhood. You have schools and buildings in your neighborhood. Think about all the things you have that are special to you in your neighborhood. As you imagine your neighborhood, you come across some litter on the ground. Do you see another opportunity to be God's partner? What can you do? Think about how you feel when you do something to help your neighborhood. Imagine how your helpfulness makes your neighbors feel. How do you feel about yourself? You have done a wonderful job. You have been a partner with God. You have done *g'milut chasadim*, an act of loving-kindness.

Relax as you hear yourself breathe. Take a slow, deep breath and feel your body relax. When you are ready you can slowly open your eyes, and without talking, just look at me so I know you are prepared to return to class.

Welcoming Guests

Introduction

The Torah is the source of many of our Jewish traditions. In this lesson, students will read the story from the Book of Genesis about Abraham welcoming the three strangers and learn about the mitzvah of *hachnasat orchim*, "hospitality." At some point in our lives, we all experience how it feels to be a "stranger"—for example, when we enroll in a new school where we don't know anybody, join a new community, move to a new neighborhood, or start a new job—and we know how important it is when someone reaches out to us and makes us feel welcome. The Jewish value of *hachnasat orchim* is about "welcoming guests" or "welcoming strangers" into our midst. This is an act of *g'milut chasadim* that students can identify with and can perform at school, on the playground, and in their homes. During the role-playing activity, teachers should use the "freeze" technique in which the actors are told to stop while performing and are then replaced by other actors. This way, all students will have an opportunity to take part in this fun activity.

Enduring Understanding

➤ We have a responsibility to perform acts of *g'milut chasadim* to make the world a better, holier place.

Essential Questions

1. Why do we do acts of *g'milut chasadim*?

2. What difference does it make if we do *g'milut chasadim*?

3. How can we learn about *g'milut chasadim* from the Torah?

Evidence of Understanding

- Students will identify acts of *g'milut chasadim* found in stories from the Torah and other Jewish sources.

- Students will identify opportunities to do acts of *g'milut chasadim.*

- Students will do personal acts of *g'milut chasadim* by carrying out a specific project planned by the teacher.

- The class will experience an act of *g'milut chasadim,* reflect on it, and analyze its impact on both the doer and the receiver.

New Vocabulary

B'ruchim habaim!	Welcome! Expression for greeting (and blessing) arriving guests
hachnasat orchim	The mitzvah of feeding and housing guests (particularly on Shabbat)
Heiveinu Shalom Aleichem	*lit.* "May peace come to all of you." A traditional Jewish folk song
hospitality	The welcoming (hospitable) reception of guests

Materials and Resources

- A CD or tape recorder

- Music for *Heiveinu Shalom Aleichem,* on tape or CD

- Some basic costumes for the teacher who will have to dress up like Abraham or Sarah, and a few cushions and rugs to recreate Abraham's desert tent

- Useful resources for the teachers include:

  Isaacs, Ronald. *Exploring Jewish Ethics and Values* (Hoboken, NJ: KTAV, 1999), pp. 20–24.

  Kadden, Barbara and Kadden, Bruce. *Teaching Mitzvot: Concepts, Values and Activities* (Denver: ARE Publications, 1988), pp. 111–114.

  Rosman, Steven. *Sedrah Stories: A Torah Companion* (New York: UAHC Press, 1989), pp. 12–14.

  Steinbock, Steven. *Torah: the Growing Gift.* New York: UAHC Press, 1994.

The Text

The following biblical text is taken from *The Torah: A Modern Commentary*, W. G. Plaut ed. (New York: UAHC Press, 1981), and is meant for the teacher only. A simplified version of this story can be found on page 224, or teachers can choose to hand out copies of "Revelation" in *Torah: The Growing Gift*, by Steven E. Steinbock (New York: UAHC Press, 1994), p. 35.

> 2] Looking up, he [Abraham] saw three men standing near him. As soon as he saw them, he ran for the entrance of the tent to greet them and, bowing to the ground, 3] he said, "My lords, if it please you, do not go on past your servant. 4] Let a little water be brought; bathe your feet and recline under the tree. 5] and let me fetch a morsel of bread that you may refresh yourselves; then go on—seeing that you have come your servant's way." They replied, "Do as you have said."
>
> 6] Abraham hastened into the tent to Sarah, and said, "Quick, three measures of choice flour! Knead and make cakes!" 7] Then Abraham ran to the herd, took a calf, tender and choice, and gave it to a servant-boy, who hastened to prepare it. 8] He took curds and milk and the calf that had been prepared, and set these before them; and he waited on them under the tree as they ate.

Genesis 18:2-8

ACTIVITY PLAN

I.   Set Induction

Arrange the classroom in a way that recreates the tent of Abraham with four open sides. Use sheets and carpets on the floor. Dress up like Abraham or Sarah. Welcome the students into the tent. Invite them to remove their shoes. Wash several students' feet. Offer them refreshments. In the background, play the song *Heiveinu Shalom Aleichem* on a tape recorder. Explain that today the class is going to learn what the Torah teaches us about welcoming guests.

Alternative Set Induction

Take students into the sanctuary and take out the Torah. Talk about how special it is, what it contains (stories, laws) and how the stories of the Torah can teach us how God wants us to behave. (If possible, have Torah rolled to portion *Vayeira*, Genesis 18:2-8.)

II. Learning Activities

The Story of Abraham, Sarah, and their Guests

1. Have students listen to the story of the hospitality of Abraham and Sarah from *Torah: The Growing Gift* (see p. …).

2. Ask them questions about the story and about Abraham and Sarah's hospitality.

- What does this story from the Torah teach us about how we should treat visitors?

- Why did the tent have four sides? Why was the tent open?

- What did Abraham and Sarah do to welcome their guests?

- Why did they wash their guests' feet?

- How did the guests get there?

- How did the guests feel?

- Why did Abraham and Sarah invite their visitors to have something to eat?

- How is this an example of *g'milut chasadim*?

3. Explain to the students that this act of *g'milut chasadim* has a special name in Hebrew. It is the Jewish value of *hachnasat orchim*—welcoming guests.

Role-Playing Activity

1. Ask the students questions about how they prepare for guests in their homes.

- When you have guests visiting your home, what do you do to prepare for your guests?

- What do you do when your guests arrive to make them feel at home?

- What do you need to think about when you have guests in your home?

- What is the difference between being a guest and a host? How do you feel as a guest, and how do you feel as a host?

- Have you ever felt strange while visiting someone else's home? What kinds of things make you feel better?

- How is being a good host an act of *g'milut chasadim*, of personal loving-kindness?

2. Have students take turns role-playing "welcoming guests" and "being a guest."

Song

One of the ways to welcome people is through music. Teach the students the tune and lyrics of *Heiveinu Shalom Aleichem* as a song to welcome guests.

Heiveinu Shalom Aleichem[1]

Peace unto you!

III. CONCLUSION

- Create a *hachnasat orchim* planning sheet for families to use next time they prepare to welcome guests.

- If a Shabbat box is sent home with different students each week, include a *hachnasat orchim* planning sheet.

- Gather the students in a circle. In a bowl, have words written on cards or strips of paper. Each student can draw a card and tell how he or she could use that word to welcome guests.

---

[1] *The Complete Shireinu.* New York: Transcontinental Music Publications, 2001; p. 85.

Word Cards for Concluding Activity

FLOWERS	FOOD	CHOCOLATES	MUSIC
PLACE CARDS	DECORATIONS	NAME TAGS	BROOM
VACUUM	TOYS	LEMONADE	COOK
ENTERTAIN	CLEAN UP	COOKIES	SIGN

Hachnasat Orchim Planning Sheet Sample

What will we do to prepare our house for our guests?

_____

What will make our home look beautiful for our guests?

_____

What special things do we need to make or buy for our guests?

_____

How should we act to make our guests comfortable?

_____

Abraham, Sarah, and their Guests

One day, Abraham was sitting outside his tent when he saw three men standing near him. As soon as he saw them, he ran to welcome them. "Please stop here for a while and visit. You must be very hot after your journey through the desert. Let me get some water for you to bathe your feet while you rest under the tree. And let me get you some food so that you can eat something before you continue on your journey." The three men agreed.

Abraham hurried into the tent and said to Sarah, "Quick, get some flour and make some cakes." Then he ran to the herd of cattle, took a calf and gave it to a servant-boy who hurried to prepare it. When everything was ready, he set all the food before his guests. Abraham waited on them under the tree as they ate.

Based on the Book of Genesis 18:1–8

Date_____

Dear Parents:

Today your child learned about the Jewish value of welcoming guests—Hachnasat Orchim. This is one way to do g'milut chasadim (personal acts of loving-kindness). In order to make a connection from our classroom to your home, I am sending home a short and simple family activity-the Hachnasat Orchim Planning Sheet. The premise of the activity is to teach your child that welcoming guests takes some planning and preparation. Please help your child fill out the form with the thought in mind of having a guest visit your home in the future. You will notice that one question asks about things you will need to make or buy for your guests. This does not mean that you have to literally present guests with gifts! It is intended to teach sensitivity about particular needs of guests-is there a food the guest can't eat or needs to eat? If the guest is an infant, a senior, a teen or anything in between, what accommodations must be considered?

Thank you for your help and participation with this family activity. We hope it will bring you closer as a family, and will enable you to share in our Jewish values of g'milut chasadim.

Sincerely,

_____

Taking Action

Introduction

Now that the students have been introduced to the concept of *g'milut chasadim* and have explored some of the possible demonstrations of loving-kindness, it is their turn to experience firsthand *g'milut chasadim*! The research that is done during this lesson is meant to prepare for a fun and interesting class field trip to a communal agency, where students will concretely experience *g'milut chasadim*. This outing should take place over the following few weeks. If a field trip is not feasible, this lesson offers teachers an alternative activity through which students can still do practical *g'milut chasadim*: they will choose a communal agency and make gifts to be distributed there, thus helping a good cause.

Through this lesson students will have an opportunity to learn about various agencies within their community that could benefit from their acts of loving-kindness. Teachers should identify beforehand three agencies that students could visit (e.g., retirement homes, food banks, animal shelters, hospitals, etc.) and obtain brochures or written materials from these places whenever possible. Invite parent volunteers or agency representatives to join you in conducting this lesson and to help facilitate the research activity. (These volunteers should be knowledgeable and/or prepared in advance with information about the given communal centers.)

Enduring Understanding

➤ We have a responsibility to perform acts of *g'milut chasadim* to make the world a better, holier place.

Essential Questions

1. Why do we do acts of *g'milut chasadim*?

2. What difference does it make if we do *g'milut chasadim*?

3. How can *g'milut chasadim* make the world a better, holier place?

Evidence of Understanding

- Students identify opportunities to do acts of *g'milut chasadim*.

- Students will plan and carry out a project that requires them to do personal acts of *g'milut chasadim*.

New Vocabulary

communal agencies   Organizations that help meet community needs. Examples of communal agencies are United Way and the Jewish federation (United Jewish Communitites)

personal endeavor   An action that an individual can accomplish

Materials and Resources

- Brochures or written materials from a number of agencies in the community

- Parent volunteers or agency representatives to help facilitate the research activity (These people must be knowledgeable and/or prepared in advance with information about the various agencies.)

- If a field trip is planned, the teacher should send a note to the students' parents explaining the project and giving details about the field trip.

The Text

"No one should let a day pass without doing a specific act of loving-kindness, whether by giving money or by a personal action."

Isaiah Horowitz (sixteenth-century Polish Jewish ethicist)

ACTIVITY PLAN

I. Set Induction

The teacher dresses up as a detective (hat, magnifying glass, trench coat, and note pad). The teacher invites the students to be detective assistants by investigating communal agencies where they can do acts of *g'milut chasadim.* The students' task is to find out as much as they can about each agency.

II.   LEARNING ACTIVITIES

Research Activity

1. Identify three agencies from your community that the students could visit and/or for which they could do a personal act of *g'milut chasadim* (e.g., retirement home, food bank, animal shelter, hospital, etc.). Obtain brochures or written materials from these places if possible.

2. Set up three stations, with a parent volunteer or an agency representative at each.

3. Break the class up into small groups and give each group a clipboard with the "Detective's Questionnaire." The students will interview the parent or agency representative at each station and fill out the questionnaire.

> ### Sample "Detective's Questionnaire"
>
> 1. Name of agency
> 2. What does this agency/place do to help others?
> 3. How could we help your agency do acts of *g'milut chasadim*?

4. Gather the students together and have them report on their findings.

5. Ask the following questions:

   Why is this agency important?

   If this agency didn't exist, what would happen?

   What can our class do to help this agency?

6. If a field trip is planned, ask the following:

   What act(s) of *g'milut chasadim* could we do at this agency?

   What difference will our acts of *g'milut chasadim* make to others?

Preparation for Field Trip

(See "Alternative Preparation" if no field trip is planned)

1. Tell the students that they are going to have the opportunity to go to one of these places for a *g'milut chasadim* field trip. As a group, decide on the agency or agencies to visit.

2. Let each student have a say in the selection.

3. Once the choice has been made, ask: What do we need to do in preparation for a visit to this agency?

4. Brainstorm a list of the items that need to be collected or the preparation needed prior to the visit. Write all ideas on the chalkboard.

Preparation Activities

NOTE: It may be necessary to use additional class time for these activities.

- Students can choose to a) learn a song that they will perform on their visit; b) create a skit that they will perform on their visit; c) create a card or gift that they will distribute on their visit; or d) make posters asking other classes to help collect items (clothing, non-perishable food items, etc.) prior to the visit.

- Send home a note to the parent(s) with details about the field trip and a permission form.

Alternative Preparation

(If no field trip is planned)

1. Tell the students that they are going to have the opportunity to do *g'milut chasadim* for one of these agencies. As a group decide on the agency or agencies to help.

2. Let each student have a say in the selection.

3. Once the choice has been made, ask: What kind of things could we do to help this agency?

4. Brainstorm a list of the items that could be collected or the things that could be made. Write all ideas on the chalkboard. (Examples: make food baskets, make challah covers, decorate cards, picture frames, collect blankets, baby items, etc.)

5. Tell the students that during the next class, they will be making these items to send to the agencies they have chosen to help. Arrange for delivery of their gifts to the agencies.

III. CONCLUSION

Gather students in circle and remind them of the quote from Polish Jewish ethicist Isaiah Horowitz: "No one should let a day pass without doing a specific act of loving-kindness, whether by giving money or by a personal action." Ask them to answer the following questions:

What do you think he meant by that?

What are some ways our project can help us fulfill this teaching?

How can our project help us make our world a better, holier place?

Reflections on Doing G'milut Chasadim

Introduction

This lesson serves as a follow-up to the field trip (or to the alternative in-class activities) recommended in the previous lesson, "Taking Action." It will provide teacher and students with the opportunity to reflect on their *g'milut chasadim* experiences. This lesson's goal is to make the students understand and recognize that their personal actions have an impact on themselves and on others, and that it is within their power to make a positive difference in the world.

Enduring Understanding

➤ We have a responsibility to perform acts of *g'milut chasadim* to make the world a better, holier place.

Essential Questions

1. Why do we do acts of *g'milut chasadim*?

2. What difference does it make if we do *g'milut chasadim*?

3. How can *g'milut chasadim* make the world a better, holier place?

Evidence of Understanding

• Students experience an act of *g'milut chasadim* and reflect on and analyze its impact on the doer, on the receiver, and on the world.

Material and Resources

- Reflection Worksheet (see sample on p. 234). This should be duplicated for each student on a large sheet of paper.

- Large sheets of chart paper for storybook

- Large poster board for cover of storybook

- Crayons and markers for illustrations

The Text

"The world wouldn't exist for even one hour without acts of loving-kindness."

Otiot, Rabbi Akiva

ACTIVITY PLAN

I. SET INDUCTION

Set at each student's desk a Reflection Worksheet (see sample). Have students complete the first sentence and the four open-ended statements. Have students use words or draw pictures to help fill in their answers to the sentences.

Last week my *g'milut chasadim* activity was _____

    I knew I was helping when_____

    I think my act of *g'milut chasadim* made a difference in the world because_____

    _____

    I think that the people or the community that I helped felt_____

    _____

    The most important thing I remember about my *g'milut chasadim* experience was_____

    _____

II. Learning Activities

Sharing Activity

Have students share their experiences, drawings, and answers to the sentences. Have them share their feelings about doing *g'milut chasadim* and making a personal difference in the lives of others.

Storybook Activity

(For classes that went on a field trip)

- Create a class storybook about *g'milut chasadim,* based on the field trip from the previous week. Develop a collaborative story using large chart paper. Have the class establish the essential elements of the story: characters, time, place, and situation.

- Write one or two sentences per sheet, leaving room for illustrations. Spread the sheets out on tables so that the students may illustrate them.

- Ask the class to help to complete "background information sheets" for the back of their class storybook to assist readers who do not have the knowledge that the students have.

Alternative Storybook Activity

(For classes that did not go on a field trip)

- Create a class storybook about *g'milut chasadim,* based on the activity from the previous week.

- Develop a collaborative story using large chart paper. Have the class establish the essential elements of the story: characters, time, place, and situation.

- Write one or two sentences per sheet, leaving room for illustrations. Have students imagine how the recipients used and enjoyed the gifts that they made for them.

- Spread the sheets out on tables so that the students may illustrate them.

- Ask the class to help to complete "background information sheets" for the back of their class storybook to assist readers who do not have the knowledge that the students have.

Example of Background Information Sheets for Storybook

G'milut chasadim is:_____

It's important to do *g'milut chasadim* because:_____

Some acts of *g'milut chasadim* that we have learned about are:_____

- Collate and laminate the book, using poster board for the cover. The class should choose an appropriate title for the book.

III. Conclusion

Gather students in a circle. Read the quote from Rabbi Akiva that is written on the chalkboard. Ask the students to explain in their own words what they think Rabbi Akiva meant. Ask them to give examples of how their storybook reflects Rabbi Akiva's idea.

Students can present the storybook at a school assembly, or during all-school *t'filah,* or at a congregational worship service. They may donate the book to the temple library.

Sample Reflection Worksheet

Last week my *g'milut chasadim* activity was_____
_____

I knew I was helping when_____
_____

I think my act of *g'milut chasadim* made a difference in
the world because_____
_____

I think that the people or the community that I helped
felt_____
_____

The most important thing I remember about my *g'milut
chasadim* experience is_____
_____

Planning a
G'milut Chasadim Simchah

Introduction

This lesson wraps up the entire second-grade unit on *g'milut chasadim*. Just as we celebrate different milestones in our lives (birthdays, anniversaries, graduation, etc.), we also celebrate the completion of our study of *g'milut chasadim*. This lesson encourages the students to take what they have learned about *g'milut chasadim* during the year and apply it to the planning of their closing celebration. Everyone loves a party, but this party will be one they'll never forget!

Enduring Understanding

➢ We have a responsibility to perform acts of *g'milut chasadim* to make the world a better, holier place.

Essential questions

1. How can we bring acts of *g'milut chasadim* into our celebrations (*smachot*)?

2. What difference does it make if we do *g'milut chasadim?*

Evidence of Understanding

• Students identify opportunities to do acts of *g'milut chasadim*.

• Class will plan and carry out a project, in the course of which students will be able to do personal acts of *g'milut chasadim*.

New Vocabulary

Chazak, chazak v'nitchazeik　　　"Be strong, be strong, and may you be strengthened!"

simchah (pl. *simchot*)　　　Hebrew word for celebration

Material and Resources

- Music for "*Chazak, chazak v'nitchazeik.*" Teachers can use the song "Chazak Chazak," music and lyrics by Julie Silver, in *The Complete Shireinu* (New York: Transcontinental Music Publications, 2001), pp. 45–46

- Construction paper, markers, scissors

- Picture frames

- Puzzle boards

The Text

חֲזַק חֲזַק וְנִתְחַזֵּק

Chazak, chazak v'nitchazeik

Be strong, be strong, and may you be strengthened!

ACTIVITY PLAN

I. SET INDUCTION

- Talk about what makes birthdays special.

- Parties are a way to celebrate special milestones. Ask the students to name other events they celebrate besides birthdays.

- Teach them the Hebrew word for Jewish celebration: *Simchah*.

- Ask students to think of ways in which they can incorporate some of the ideas and concepts learned about *g'milut chasadim* into their future celebrations—birthday parties or Jewish events (*Simchah*).

- Now that study of *g'milut chasadim* has been completed, invite the class to plan a *G'milut Chasadim Simchah* to honor their successful learning. (Choose a day and time for this event.)

Chai: Learning for Jewish Life   **Planning a *G'milut Chasadim Simchah***   237

II. LEARNING ACTIVITIES

Preparation

List the elements of a party on the chalkboard. Ask the students to think about what they might do that would make this party a "*g'milut chasadim* party"?

Invitations

- Who should be invited? How would that be an act of *g'milut chasadim*?

- What should the invitation say? How would that be an act of *g'milut chasadim*?

Guests

- How should we greet our guests? How would that be an act of *g'milut chasadim*?

- How can we make our guests feel comfortable? How would that be an act of *g'milut chasadim*?

Food

- What could we do with food that would help us to do an act of *g'milut chasadim*?

- What could our guests do?

Presents

- If this is going to be a *g'milut chasadim* party, who should receive gifts?

Activities

- What kind of activities might we do that would remind us about *g'milut chasadim*?

Simchah Party Time!

Gather the class and help them figure out a good day and time for their *G'milut Chasadim Simchah*. Divide students into groups and have them do the following activities based on the previous discussion:

1. Design invitations.

2. Create a list of instructions to the class for greeting guests.

3. Plan ways to do an act of *g'milut chasadim* related to food. (For example, baking extra cookies and delivering them to someone who is sick or to elderly people, or asking guests to bring in a non-perishable food item to be donated to a food-bank.)

4. Activities: Create several *g'milut chasadim* activities based on familiar games (pin the fruit on the *g'milut chasadim* tree; hopscotch over a board that has acts of *g'milut chasadim* written in the squares).

5. Presents: Create gifts (such as picture frames containing some of the texts that have been used throughout the *G'milut Chasadim* course to give residents of an old age home; a *g'milut chasadim* picture puzzle done on cardboard puzzle board to be given to students at a hospital or shelter).

III. CONCLUSION

• Explain to students that Jewish tradition has a special way of celebrating the end of a study period. For example, there is a special blessing that celebrates the completion of the reading of a book of Torah. Write the blessing on the chalkboard and talk about its meaning.

חֲזַק חֲזַק וְנִתְחַזֵּק

Chazak, Chazak, V'nitchazeik

Be strong, be strong, and may you be strengthened!

• Ask the students how this blessing for the completion of Torah study could be applied to their completion of the study of *g'milut chasadim.* Play the song "Chazak Chazak" by Julie Silver and sing it all together.

Useful Bibliography for *G'milut Chasadim*

Let's Discover Mitzvot: Welcome Guests, New Jersey: Behrman House, 2001.

Geras, Adele, ed. "A Mensch Is Someone Special," by Phyllis Rose Eisenberg in *A Treasury of Jewish Stories*. New York: Kingfisher, 1996.

Kadden, Barbara and Bruce Kadden. *Teaching Mitzvot: Concepts, Values and Activities.* Denver: ARE Publications, 1988; pp. 111–114.

Rosman, Steven. *Sedrah Stories: A Torah Companion*. New York: UAHC Press, 1989; pp. 12–14.

Sasso, Sandy Eisenberg, *God's Paintbrush*. Woodstock, Vt.: Jewish Lights, 1992.

Steinbock, Steven. *Torah: The Growing Gift*. New York: UAHC Press, 1994.

Syme, Deborah Shayne, *Partners*. New York: UAHC Press, 1990.

"Chazak, Chazak," music and lyrics by Julie Silver, in *The Complete Shireinu*. New York: Transcontinental Music Publications, 2001; pp. 45–46.